SYRIA 2016 HUMAN RIGHTS REPORT

Note: This report was updated 3/29/17; see Appendix F: Errata for more information.

EXECUTIVE SUMMARY

President Bashar Asad has ruled the Syrian Arab Republic since 2000. The constitution mandates the primacy of Baath Party leaders in state institutions and society, and Asad and Baath party leaders dominated all three branches of government. The 2014 presidential election won by Asad and the geographically limited parliamentary elections in April won by the Baath Party took place in an environment of widespread government coercion. The results did not reflect the unimpeded or uncoerced will of the electorate. In government-controlled areas, Asad made key decisions with counsel from a small number of military and security advisors, ministers, and senior members of the ruling Baath Party. The government routinely violated the human rights of its citizens as major conflict enveloped the country.

The government maintained control over its uniformed military, police, and state security forces but did not maintain effective control over foreign and local paramilitary organizations. These included Hizballah and the Islamic Revolutionary Guard Corps; nonuniformed progovernment militias, such as the National Defense Forces; the Bustan Charitable Association; or "shabiha," which often acted autonomously without oversight or direction from the government.

The government's use of lethal force to quell peaceful civil protests calling for reform and democracy in 2011 precipitated a civil war in 2012. The civil war continued during the year. The government maintained control over most areas of the coastal governorates and in areas in and around Damascus. It regularly attacked areas with significant opposition presence. By year's end progovernment forces had retaken eastern Aleppo City. Different opposition groups with varying ideologies and goals controlled several parts of the north and areas in the Golan Heights, in many cases establishing new or reconstituted governance structures, including irregularly constituted courts. Most notably, the terrorist organization Da'esh took control of the eastern governorates Deir al-Zour and Raqqa in 2014. Subsequently, Da'esh announced the establishment of what it called an Islamic "caliphate" with the city of Raqqa as its capital. Da'esh also maintained limited presence in other governorates in the north and south and around Damascus. Control over other areas of the country remained contested, including the northeastern areas dominated by ethnic Kurds and the Turkish border region. Beginning in August, Turkey launched Operation Euphrates Shield with the declared intention of preventing Da'esh, the PKK, PYD, and YPG from establishing a "terror corridor" on its southern border.

The Asad government and its supporters reportedly continued to use indiscriminate and deadly force against civilians, conducting air and ground-based military assaults on cities, residential areas, and civilian infrastructure. Attacks against schools, hospitals, mosques, churches, synagogues, water stations, bakeries, markets, civil defense forces centers, and houses were common throughout the country. In April, UN Special Envoy for Syria Staffan di Mistura estimated that the fighting had resulted in the deaths of more than 400,000 persons since 2011. The humanitarian situation reached severe levels. As of December 2015, there were more than 4.8 million Syrian refugees registered with the Office of the UN High Commissioner for Refugees (UNHCR) in neighboring countries and 6.1 million persons displaced internally as of August. The government frequently blocked access for humanitarian assistance and removed items such as medical supplies from convoys headed to civilian areas, particularly areas held by opposition groups.

The most egregious human rights violations stemmed from the state's widespread disregard for the safety and well-being of its citizens. This manifested itself in a complete denial of citizens' ability to choose their government peacefully, a breakdown in law enforcement's ability to protect the majority of citizens from state and nonstate violence, and the use of violence against civilians and civilian institutions. The government arbitrarily and unlawfully killed, tortured, and detained persons on a wide scale. Government and progovernment forces conducted attacks on civilians in hospitals, residential areas, schools, and settlements for internally displaced persons (IDPs) and refugee camps; these attacks included bombardment with improvised explosive devices, commonly referred to as "barrel bombs." During the year the United Nations reported increased use of incendiary weapons, including napalm and white phosphorous, as well as chlorine gas. The government continued the use of torture and rape, including of children. It used the massacre of civilians, as well as their forced displacement, rape, starvation, and protracted sieges that occasionally forced local surrenders, as military tactics. Government authorities detained without access to fair trial tens of thousands of individuals, including those associated with nongovernmental organizations (NGOs), human rights activists, journalists, relief workers, religious figures, and medical providers. Government authorities rigorously denied citizens the right to a fair public trial and the ability to exercise civil liberties and freedoms of expression, movement, peaceful assembly, and association.

Additional human rights problems included: restrictions on religious observance and movement throughout the country; abuse of refugees and stateless persons; prevention of NGOs and individual activists, especially those working on civil society and democracy matters, from organizing; restrictions on access for medical providers to persons in critical need; rampant governmental corruption; violence and societal discrimination against women and minorities; and restrictions on workers' rights.

Impunity was pervasive and deeply embedded in the security forces and elsewhere in the government, since the government did not attempt to investigate, punish, arrest, or prosecute officials who violated human rights. The government often sheltered and encouraged those in its ranks to commit abuses.

Government-linked paramilitary groups reportedly engaged in frequent violations and abuses, including massacres, indiscriminate killings, kidnapping of civilians, arbitrary detentions, and rape as a war tactic. Government-affiliated militias, including the terrorist organization Lebanese Hizballah, supported by Iran, repeatedly targeted civilians.

Some opposition groups, including armed terrorist groups such as the al-Qaida-linked Jabhat al-Nusra (renamed Jabhat Fatah al-Sham in July after the group claimed to split from al-Qaida), also committed a wide range of abuses, including those involving massacres, bombings, and kidnappings; unlawful detention; torture; executions; and forced evacuations from homes based on sectarian identity. Da'esh committed massive abuses in the territory it controlled in Raqqa and Deir al-Zour governorates, according to numerous human rights organizations, the media, UN reports, and Da'esh itself. According to the media and eyewitnesses, these abuses included mass executions; stoning of women and men accused of adultery; crucifixions of civilians; public executions of foreign journalists, aid workers, "blasphemers" (described as those Da'esh defined as insufficiently Muslim or those accused of undefined acts of blasphemy), and those suspected of "being gay." Human trafficking and the forcible recruitment and use of children in the conflict increased. There were reports of systematic rape and forced marriages of women and girls for sexual slavery among Da'esh fighters. Secretary Kerry stated on March 17 that in his judgment, Da'esh was responsible for genocide against groups in areas under its control, including Yezidis, Christians, and Shia Muslims, and was also responsible for crimes against humanity and ethnic cleansing directed at these same groups and in some cases also against Sunni Muslims, Kurds, and other minorities.

There were also reports of Kurdish forces displacing residents after liberating areas from Da'esh. Amnesty International (AI) last reported such actions in October 2015. During the year unconfirmed reports from Syrian human rights groups indicated that Kurdish authorities arrested local civil council leaders, journalists, and other civilians.

Section 1. Respect for the Integrity of the Person, Including Freedom from:

a. Arbitrary Deprivation of Life and other Unlawful or Politically Motivated Killings

There were numerous reports the government and its agents committed arbitrary or unlawful killings in relation to the civil war (see section 1.g.).

The government continued its use of helicopters and airplanes to conduct aerial bombardment and shelling. In the first half of the year, government forces reportedly indiscriminately dropped more than six thousand barrel bombs, killing large numbers of civilians.

The Syrian Network for Human Rights (SNHR) reported the government killed 6,924 civilians from January through November. Nongovernment forces, including both extremist groups such as Da'esh and nonextremist rebel groups, also committed arbitrary or unlawful killings, with the SNHR reporting that Da'esh was responsible for 1,397 civilian deaths. The SNHR also reported that during the same period, Russian forces killed 2,844 civilians in support of government operations (see section 1.g.). The SNHR reported that armed opposition groups killed 900 civilians.

b. Disappearance

The UN Commission of Inquiry on Syria (COI) reported the number of forced disappearances remained high. The majority of disappearances reported by activists, human rights observers, and international NGOs appeared to be politically motivated. In August the SNHR attributed 96 percent of the estimated 75,000 forced disappearances to the government. The government reportedly targeted critics, specifically journalists, medical personnel, antigovernment protesters, their families, and associates. The COI reported that government forces continued to engage in mass arrests of wounded persons attempting to leave besieged areas at checkpoints and in areas that fell under their control. Following the surrender of towns such as Darayaa and Moadimiyah after years of siege and starvation tactics, the government evacuated residents by buses escorted by the Syrian Arab Red Crescent (SARC). The government gave civilians the choice of relocating nearby, but the government required opposition fighters to take personal weapons and relocate to Idlib governorate. The government reportedly arrested men of fighting age, especially Sunni, perceived to be associated with opposition groups. The COI noted that the families of disappeared persons often feared to approach authorities to inquire about the whereabouts of their relatives; those who did so had to pay large bribes to learn the whereabouts of relatives or faced systematic refusal by authorities to disclose information about the fate of disappeared individuals. The COI reported that the large number of missing men contributed to a sharp rise in female-headed households and increased the number of female IDPs and refugees.

AI reported that the government provided no further information on the thousands of individuals who had disappeared since the start of the conflict or the 17,000 persons who had disappeared since the 1970s. Human rights groups' estimates of the total number of disappearances since 2011 varied widely, but all estimates pointed to disappearances as a pervasive and common practice. AI estimated that authorities forcibly had abducted more than 65,000 persons since the start of the conflict, including 58,000 civilians and seven thousand members of armed groups. The SNHR likewise reported that it possessed a list of more than 117,000 detainees from 2011 to the end of November. A number of prominent political prisoners remained missing (see section 1.e.). The SNHR reported that government forces and pro-government militias were responsible for 5,228 cases of arbitrary arrest of men, women, and children from January through November.

Nongovernment armed extremist groups conducted kidnappings, particularly in the northern areas, targeting religious leaders, aid workers, suspected government affiliates, journalists, and activists. According to the COI, reports of enforced disappearances in territory held by Da'esh, particularly the cities of Raqqa and Aleppo, also increased.

These groups also abducted individuals (see section 1.g.).

c. Torture and Other Cruel, Inhuman, or Degrading Treatment or Punishment

The law prohibits torture and other cruel, inhuman, or degrading treatment or punishment, and the penal code provides up to three years' imprisonment for violations. Activists, the COI, and local NGOs reported thousands of credible cases of government authorities engaging in frequent torture to punish perceived opponents, including during interrogations. Observers reported most cases of torture or mistreatment occurred in detention centers operated by each of the government's security service branches. Human Rights Watch (HRW) and the COI reported regular use of detention and torture of government opponents at checkpoints and facilities run by the air force, Political Security Division, General Security Directorate, and Military Intelligence Directorate. They identified specific detention facilities where torture occurred, including the Mezzeh airport detention facility, Military Security Branches 215, 227, 235, 248, and 291, Adra and Sednaya prisons, the Harasta Air Force Intelligence Branch, Harasta Military Hospital, Mezzeh Military Hospital 601, and Tishreen Military Hospital. The COI also reported the Counterterrorism Court (CTC) and field military courts' reliance on forced confessions and information acquired through torture to obtain convictions. A large number of torture victims reportedly died in custody; the SNHR reported that 12,679 individuals died due to torture between early 2011 and May; 99 percent of these cases occurred in government facilities between May 2011 and June (see section 1.a.).

Activists cited thousands of credible cases of security forces abusing and torturing prisoners and detainees and maintained that many instances of abuse went unreported. Some declined to allow reporting of their names or details of their cases due to fear of government reprisal.

In 2013 a defector from the government, a former military police photographer known as "Caesar," smuggled out thousands of photographs from inside government detention centers dating from 2011 to 2013. According to a December 2015 HRW report, a review and forensic analysis by HRW of 28,707 of the photographs identified at least 6,786 deceased detainees--including children-- showing signs of torture and severe malnourishment. The COI asserted the methods of torture and the conditions of detention, as evidenced in the photographs in Military Hospital No. 601 in Damascus, supported the commission's longstanding findings of systematic torture and deaths of detainees.

The COI noted that during the year torture methods remained consistent. These included beatings on the head, bodies, and soles of feet ("falaqua") with wooden and metal sticks, hoses, cables, belts, whips, and wires. Authorities also reportedly sexually assaulted detainees; administered electric shocks, including to their genitals; burned detainees with cigarettes; and placed them in stress positions for prolonged periods of time. A substantial number of male detainees reported being handcuffed and then suspended from the ceiling or a wall by their wrists for hours.

Other reported methods of physical torture included removing nails and hair, stabbings, and cutting off body parts, including ears and genitals. Numerous human rights organizations reported other forms of torture, including forcing objects into the rectum and vagina, hyperextending the spine, and putting the victim onto the frame of a wheel and whipping exposed body parts. Additionally, officers reportedly continued the practice of "shabeh," in which they stripped detainees naked, hung them for prolonged periods from the ceiling, and administered electrical shocks. In August, AI and the Human Rights Data Analysis Group published a detailed account of 12,270 documented killings in Sednaya Prison that included detailed depictions of "welcome party" beatings, "security check" rapes, and drawings of various configurations of physical torture. Detainees emphasized that authorities not only beat them during interrogations but that prison guards also beat them in their cells.

Medical professionals reported witnessing persons burned alive in government detention facilities. State authorities reportedly issued fabricated death certificates with the apparent intent of disguising the cause and location of death and of preventing any official record of the use of torture. Numerous NGOs asserted that the practice of returning corpses to family members to announce their deaths continued, and corpses exhibited signs of torture.

The use of psychological torture by the government also reportedly increased. One commonly reported practice was detention of victims overnight in cells with corpses of previous victims. The SNHR reported that psychological torture methods included forcing prisoners to witness the rape of other prisoners, threatening the rape of family members (in particular female family members), forcing prisoners to undress, and insulting prisoners' beliefs.

Various NGOs, including HRW, AI, and the SNHR, continued to report widespread instances of rape and sexual abuse, including of minors. The COI reported receiving reports of interrogators raping and sexually abusing male detainees held in Branch 285 of the General Directorate of Intelligence in Damascus. The COI also reported that government personnel raped and used other forms of sexual violence against women in detention facilities as well as at checkpoints. A COI report noted that authorities subjected prisoners to threats of sexual violence against their female relatives while in custody.

Reports from multiple UN and NGO sources indicated the number of cases of rape and other extreme sexual violence against women during the year ranged from the high hundreds to thousands. According to the COI, the government and affiliated militias systematically perpetrated rape and other inhuman attacks against civilian populations in Deir al-Zour, Dara'a, Hama, Damascus, and Tartus governorates. Detention centers were the most common location for abuse. In several interviews with the COI, former female prisoners reported being forced to perform oral sex on interrogators and witnessing the rape of other inmates. In AI's report on Sednaya Prison, both female and male prisoners reported guards and interrogators raped them as part of "security checks" or in conjunction with other physical torture. Attacks also occurred during military raids and at checkpoints. These cases of mostly government-sponsored violence included instances in which multiple attackers, usually soldiers and shabiha, reportedly gang-raped women in their homes, sometimes in front of family members. Such incidents reportedly took place in private homes or in situations of formal and informal custody. The COI also reported rape of and sexual assault on men and boys.

There were widespread reports government security forces engaged in abuse and inhuman treatment of prisoners. According to the COI, most were civilians initially held at checkpoints or taken prisoner during military incursions. While the majority of accounts concerned male detainees, there were increased reports of female detainees suffering abuse in government custody. The frequency, duration, and severity of the reported abuse suggested victims' sustained long-term psychological and physical damage.

The COI reported that, beginning in 2011 and continuing through the year, security forces subjected detainees to mistreatment in military hospitals, often obstructing medical care or exacerbating existing injuries as a technique in abuse and interrogation. There were multiple reports of deaths in custody at the Mezzeh airport detention facility, Military Security Branches 215 and 235, and Sednaya Prison. Authorities consistently directed families of detainees seeking information to the Qaboun Military Police and Tishreen Military Hospital. In most cases authorities reportedly did not return the bodies of deceased detainees to their families. In January authorities confirmed the death of a paramedic, Amer Safaf, in Sednaya Prison with his body showing signs of torture after government forces arrested him in 2012.

There continued to be a significant number of reports of exceptionally brutal cases of abuse of children by the government. The COI noted regular reports of detention and torture of children under the age of 13, in some cases as young as 11, in government detention facilities. Officials reportedly targeted and tortured children because of their familial relations, or assumed relationships, with political dissidents, members of the armed opposition, and activist groups. The UN special representative for children and armed conflict reported that child detainees, largely boys, including those as young as 14, suffered similar or identical methods of torture practiced on adults, including electric shocks, beatings, stress positions, threats, and acts of sexual assault. According to reliable witnesses, authorities continued to hold a number of children to compel parents and other relatives associated with opposition fighters to surrender to authorities.

Although authorities held fewer women and girls in detention than men, the SNHR estimated the number of female detainees in government prisons between the beginning of the uprising in 2011 and April to be more than seven thousand. The SNHR estimated that 2,850 women remained in prison.

In 2015 the Women's International League for Peace and Freedom reported that authorities often detained women for use in bargaining with their male family members. Authorities exchanged them for weapons of armed opposition groups. Security officers also subjected women to sexual exploitation while searching for their detained family members.

Nongovernment forces, including both extremist groups such as Da'esh and nonextremist rebel groups, also engaged in physical abuse, punishment, and torture of individuals (see section 1.g.).

Prison and Detention Center Conditions

Prison and detention center conditions remained harsh and in many instances were life threatening. The government prohibited independent monitoring of prison or detention center conditions. Reports of mistreatment and abuse of prisoners were common. The COI reported that observers most often cited detention centers and prisons as locations for sexual violence and that authorities used the threat of rape as a tool to coerce confessions.

Physical Conditions: In June the SNHR reported that since 2011 it had documented the arrest of more than 117,000 individuals and estimated that authorities had detained more than 215,000 persons; the SNHR attributed 99 percent of those detentions to the government. According to HRW, released detainees consistently reported abuse and torture in detention facilities and prison conditions that often led to deaths in custody. According to the COI, government detention facilities lacked food, water, space, hygiene, and medical care. Poor conditions were so consistent that the COI concluded they reflected state policy.

According to local and international NGOs, the government held prisoners and detainees in severely cramped quarters with little or no access to toilets, hygiene, medical supplies, or adequate food. In a report from HRW in December 2015, detainees told HRW researchers that authorities used small cells measuring 21.5 square feet and intended for solitary confinement to house several prisoners. Due to the extremely crowded nature of these cells, detainees could only stand and had to take turns sleeping.

In August the COI reported that conditions in detention facilities, and specifically those run by intelligence agencies, remained abysmal. Former detainees reported lice infestations, untreated wounds, and a general lack of such basic necessities as food, water, space, hygiene, and medical care.

Reports from multiple international NGO sources suggested that there were also many informal detention sites and that authorities held thousands of prisoners in converted military bases and in civilian infrastructure, such as schools and stadiums, and in unknown locations. Activists asserted the government also housed arrested protesters in factories and vacant warehouses that were overcrowded and lacked adequate sanitary facilities. Authorities imprisoned female detainees in squalid, insect-infested cells and subjected them to torture and inhuman treatment. Medical care, if available at all, was inadequate and did not address women's medical and physiological needs.

Prior to the 2011 protests, the government usually held pretrial detainees separately from convicted prisoners. During the year, authorities commonly held juveniles, adults, pretrial detainees, and convicted prisoners together in inadequate spaces during the year. The COI reported that authorities held children as young as eight years old in prison with adults.

In some cases authorities transferred detainees from unofficial holding areas to intelligence services facilities. Detention conditions at security and intelligence service facilities continued to be the harshest, especially for political or national security prisoners. Facilities lacked proper ventilation, lighting, access to potable water or adequate food, medical staff and equipment, and sufficient sleeping quarters. According to the COI, most former detainees reported inadequate food, with some losing half their body weight while detained.

Inside prisons and detention centers, the prevalence of death from disease remained high due to unsanitary conditions and withholding medical care and medication. Local NGOs and medical professionals reported that authorities denied medical care to prisoners with pre-existing health needs, such as diabetes, asthma, and breast cancer, and denied pregnant women any medical care. Authorities retaliated against prisoners who requested attention for the sick. Released prisoners commonly reported sickness and injury resulting from such conditions. Information on conditions and care for prisoners with disabilities was unavailable.

In March inmates in Hama prison rioted in protest of inhuman treatment, torture, and killings during imprisonment. Reports from domestic human rights activists and media showed that government forces fired tear gas and positioned snipers around the prison during the revolt. In August human rights activists reported fighting between prisoners and guards in Sweida prison south of Damascus. Reports indicated that the government stormed the prison shortly thereafter, firing tear gas, severely injuring a number of prisoners, and killing at least two.

According to the COI, conditions in detention centers run by nonstate actors such as Da'esh violated international law. Detainees in Raqqa governorate reported that Da'esh held them in crowded, insect-infested cells with neither light nor bedding. Da'esh reportedly denied prisoners access to adequate food or legal counsel and prevented communication outside the facility. Da'esh appropriated former government prison facilities for its use, such as those in al-Bab and Jarablus in Aleppo governorate.

Conditions in detention centers operated by various opposition groups were not well known, but the COI and local NGOs reported accounts of arbitrary detention, torture, inhuman treatment, and abuse.

Administration: The government made no serious attempts to improve recordkeeping. There were no credible mechanisms or avenues for prisoners to complain or submit grievances, and authorities routinely failed to investigate allegations or document complaints or grievances. Activists reported there was no ombudsman to serve on behalf of prisoners and detainees. The law provides for prompt access to family members, but NGOs and families reported inconsistent application of the law, with some families waiting as long as one year to see relatives. The government continued to detain thousands of prisoners without charge and incommunicado in unknown locations.

In areas where government control was weak or nonexistent, localized corrections structures emerged. There were varied reports of control and oversight, and both civilian and religious leaders were in charge of facility administration. Former police forces or members of armed opposition groups operated facilities in areas under the control of opposition forces. Nonstate actors often did not understand due process and lacked sufficient training to run facilities.

<u>Independent Monitoring</u>: The government prohibited most independent monitoring of prison or detention center conditions, and diplomatic and consular officials had no greater access than in previous years. Some opposition forces invited the COI to visit localized facilities they administered and allowed some international human rights groups, including HRW, to visit. The International Committee of the Red Cross/Red Crescent continued to negotiate with all parties, except Da'esh, to gain access to detention centers across but was unable to gain access to any government-controlled facilities during the year.

d. Arbitrary Arrest or Detention

The constitution prohibits arbitrary arrest and detention, although a 2011 decree allows the government to detain suspects for up to 60 days without charge if suspected of "terrorism" and other related offenses. Arbitrary arrests increased according to local news sources, and several human rights organizations reported detentions in the tens of thousands. In February the COI published a report entitled "Out of Sight, Out of Mind: Deaths in Detention in the Syrian Arab Republic." The report said that "since March 2011, a countrywide pattern emerged in which civilians, mainly males above the age of 15, were arbitrarily arrested and detained by the Syrian security and armed forces or by militia acting on behalf of the government during mass arrests, house searches, at checkpoints, and in hospitals. Arrests targeted civilians perceived to be either supporting the opposition or insufficiently loyal to the government."

HRW reported the government continued to use the counterterrorism law to arrest and convict nonviolent activists on charges of aiding terrorists in trials that violated basic due process rights. Although authorities reportedly brought charges under the guise of countering violent militancy, allegations included peaceful acts such as distributing humanitarian aid, participating in protests, and documenting human rights abuses.

National security forces failed to respond to or protect large regions of the country from violence. AI reported that armed groups detained suspected government supporters, local activists, foreign journalists, aid workers, and others. The COI also reported that nonstate armed groups, including Ahrar al-Sham and Jabhat al-Nusra, took hostages, especially women and children, to force prisoner exchanges with the government or other armed groups or for ransom (see section 1.g.). Observers suspected Jabhat al-Nusra of holding foreign hostages. According to some reports, the Democratic Union Party (PYD) arbitrarily detained 36 Kurdish opposition figures in areas they controlled. Multiple reports accused the PYD or PYD-aligned forces of targeting Assyrian Christians and Yezidis for compulsory military service, seizing their assets and homes, and forcibly removing them from their land.

Role of the Police and Security Apparatus

The government's multiple security branches traditionally operated autonomously with no defined boundaries between their areas of jurisdiction. Military Intelligence and Air Force Intelligence reported to the Ministry of Defense, the Political Security Directorate reported to the Ministry of Interior, and the General Intelligence Directorate reported directly to the Office of the President. The Interior Ministry controlled the four separate divisions of police forces: emergency police, traffic police, neighborhood police, and riot police.

Government-affiliated shabiha forces reorganized and in 2013 rebranded themselves as the National Defense Forces (NDF). These groups engaged in armed conflict and arrested, detained, and tortured those suspected of supporting the opposition. The NDF integrated with government-affiliated forces. There also were other progovernment militias outside the NDF.

Impunity continued to be a widespread problem. The General Command of the Army and Armed Forces could issue arrest warrants for crimes committed by military officers, members of the internal security forces, or customs police during their normal duties; military courts must try such cases. There were no known prosecutions or convictions of police and security force personnel for abuse or corruption; however, security forces operated independently and generally outside the control of the legal system. There were no reported government actions to reform the security forces or police.

Opposition forces established irregularly constituted courts and detention facilities in areas under their control, which varied greatly in organization and adherence to judicial norms. Some groups upheld the penal code, others followed a 1996 draft Arab League Unified Penal Code based on sharia (Islamic law), while others implemented a mix of customary law and sharia. The experience, expertise, and credentialing of opposition judges and religious scholars also varied widely, and dominant armed militias in the area often subjected them to their orders.

Da'esh claimed that it based administration of justice in the territory it controlled on religious law. Da'esh purportedly authorized its police forces, known as "hisbah," to administer summary punishment for violations of Da'esh's morality code. Men faced beatings for smoking, possessing alcohol, listening to music, trading during prayer times, and not fasting during Ramadan. Da'esh punished others for accompanying "improperly dressed" female relatives.

Arrest Procedures and Treatment of Detainees

The law generally requires a warrant for arrest in criminal cases, but police often cited emergency or national security justifications for acting without a warrant, permitted under the law. Police usually brought arrested individuals to a police station for processing and detention until a trial date was set. The law stipulates that the length of time authorities may hold a person without charge is limited to 60 days, but according to various NGOs, activists, and former detainees, police held many individuals for longer periods or indefinitely. Civil and criminal defendants have the right to bail hearings and possible release from detention on their own recognizance. The legal system inconsistently applied this right, particularly with pretrial detainees. At the initial court hearing, which can be months or years after the arrest, the accused may retain an attorney at personal expense or the court may appoint an attorney, although authorities did not assure lawyers access to their clients before trial. According to local human rights organizations, denial of access to a lawyer was common.

In cases involving political or national security offenses, authorities reportedly often made arrests in secret with cases assigned in an apparently arbitrary manner to military, security, or criminal courts. The government reportedly detained suspects incommunicado for prolonged periods without charge or trial and denied them the right to a judicial determination of their pretrial detention. In most cases authorities reportedly did not inform detainees of charges against them until their arraignment, often months after their arrest. Security detainees did not have access to lawyers before or during questioning or throughout preparation and presentation of their defense. The number of suspects accused of political and national security offenses reportedly increased compared with previous years.

The government often reputedly failed to notify foreign governments when it arrested, detained, released, or deported their citizens, especially when the case involved political charges. The government also failed to provide consular access to foreign citizens known to be in its prisons and, on numerous occasions, claimed these individuals were not in their custody or even in the country.

Arbitrary Arrest: Security forces continued their previous practices and reportedly increased arbitrary arrests, but detainees had no legal redress. Reports continued of security services arresting relatives of wanted persons to pressure individuals to surrender. Police rarely issued or presented warrants or court orders before an arrest. According to reports, the security branches secretly ordered many arrests and detentions. Activists and international humanitarian organizations stated that government forces continued to conduct security raids in response to antigovernment protests throughout urban areas. In areas under government control, security forces engaged in arbitrary arrests. The SNHR reported that government forces launched widespread arrest and raid campaigns in January to force military recruitment on young men. The COI reported that authorities arbitrarily arrested men and boys over the age of 12 at some checkpoints. Often authorities cited no reason for arresting civilians.

Checkpoints operated by the government were another commonly reported location for arbitrary arrests, sometimes resulting in transfer to a long-term detention facility or disappearance. Government military and security forces reportedly arrested men at checkpoints solely for being of military age. According to the COI, there continued to be frequent accounts of enforced disappearances following arrest at checkpoints.

Multiple reports from local and international NGOs stated that the government prevented the majority of those detained from contacting their relatives or obtaining a lawyer. When authorities occasionally released detainees, it was often without any formal judicial procedures. Hundreds of detainees interviewed by human rights groups stated that they had been arrested, detained, questioned, and released after months of detention without seeing a judge or being sentenced.

The SNHR reported that Da'esh also kidnapped many individuals in areas under its control. It also alleged that PYD-affiliated Kurdish forces arrested Arab civilians, activists, and politicians and took them to unknown destinations.

<u>Pretrial Detention</u>: Lengthy pretrial detention remained a serious problem. Authorities reportedly held many detainees incommunicado for years before bringing them to trial. A shortage of available courts and lack of legal provisions for speedy trial or plea bargaining also contributed to lengthy pretrial detentions. There were numerous reported instances when the length of detention exceeded the sentence for the crime. Percentages for prison/detainee population held in pretrial detention and the length of time held were not available during the year.

<u>Detainee's Ability to Challenge Lawfulness of Detention before a Court</u>: Not all detainees have the ability to challenge the lawfulness of their detention before a court or obtain prompt release and compensation if found to have been unlawfully detained.

<u>Amnesty</u>: In February the government offered a general amnesty to any military deserters willing to surrender in 30 days after the law took effect, if they were still in the country. The law granted anyone outside the country 60 days to return to the country and surrender. The March Cessation of Hostilities statement called for the United Nations to form a committee to monitor the release of detainees periodically; however, there was no progress made on release of detainees during the year.

e. Denial of Fair Public Trial

The constitution provides for an independent judiciary, but authorities regularly subjected courts to political influence, and outcomes of cases with political context appeared predetermined.

Trial Procedures

The law presumes defendants innocent. Defendants have the right to prompt, detailed notification of the charges against them with interpretation as necessary, although authorities did not verifiably enforce this right, and a number of detainees' families mentioned that the accused were unaware of the charges facing them. Trials are public, except for those involving juveniles or sexual offenses. The law entitles defendants before civil and criminal courts to representation of their choice; the courts appoint lawyers for indigents. Defendants and their attorneys nominally have access to government-held evidence relevant to their cases. It was unknown if attorneys had adequate time and facilities to prepare a defense. Human rights lawyers noted, however, that in some politically charged cases, the government provided prosecution case files to defense lawyers that did not include any evidence. Defendants can present evidence and confront their accusers. Defendants cannot legally be compelled to testify or confess guilt, but family members and NGOs reported that torture or intimidation from judges and prosecutors sometimes elicited false confessions. Convicted persons could appeal verdicts to a provincial appeals court and ultimately to the Court of Cassation.

Not all citizens enjoyed these rights equally, in part because interpretations of religious law provide the basis for elements of family and criminal law and discriminate against women. Some personal status laws applied sharia law regardless of the religion of those involved. Additionally, news media and NGO reports suggested the government denied some, and in certain cases all, of these protections to those accused of political crimes or violence against the government. Sentences for persons accused of antigovernment activity tended to be harsh, with violent offenders and nonviolent offenders receiving similar punishments. The Violations Documentation Center (VDC) reported that the number of cases referred to the CTC exceeded 80,000 by April, two and a one-half years after it began accepting cases. According to the SNHR, the majority of those tried received five- to 20-year prison sentences. The government did not permit defendants before the CTC to have legal representation, although activists reported individuals charged under the counterterrorism law could retain attorneys to move their trial date.

In opposition-controlled areas, legal or trial procedures varied by locale. Local human rights organizations reported that local governing structures assumed these responsibilities. HRW reported that civilians administered these processes employing customary sharia laws in some cases and national laws in others. Sentencing by opposition sharia councils sometimes resulted in public executions, without an appeals process or visits by family members.

According to local NGOs, opposition-run sharia councils continued to discriminate against women, not allowing them to serve as judges or lawyers or to visit detainees.

The Aleppo Sharia Commission, associated with some armed opposition forces, operated a court system with courts on civil, criminal, military, and civilian affairs. These courts reportedly followed the Unified Arab League draft code rather than the country's legal code. In Dara'a opposition forces formed the House of Justice in 2014, building on the Unified Judicial Sharia Commission, formerly known as the Gharz Court, and making judgements on criminal activities, commercial transactions, and civil affairs.

The Supreme Sharia Court in northern rural Homs was the main coordinator for civilian issues in the area. This court was reportedly the most powerful governing body in the area and responsible for most major local decisions. The Supreme Sharia Court unified the sharia courts in Ar-Rastan, Talbiseh, and Houla. It consists of judicial experts, lawyers, and judges who regulate civil disputes. The court oversees implementation of its orders with a police force composed of local armed opposition group members, to include Jaish Tawheed, Faylaq Homs, and Ahrar al-Sham as well as local volunteers. While the court had representation from Jabhat al-Nusra, the group did not exercise significant influence over the court's decisions.

The Majles al-Shura (Consultative Council) was formed in late 2015. It includes prominent family members, notables, and influential persons in the towns of Ar-Rastan and Talbiseh. It is primarily concerned with the long-term logistical planning (such as the local ban on wheat trading with the government) and local truce negotiations with the government. The authority of the Majles varied across the Homs governorate.

In the territory it controlled, Da'esh purported to establish courts to preside over its interpretation of religious law headed by judges with unknown credentials based on an unknown selection process.

Political Prisoners and Detainees

The government detained critics and charged them with a wide range of political crimes, including terrorism. The number of political prisoners and detainees, both citizens and foreigners, was difficult to determine due to a lack of government information and because different security services maintained their own incarceration facilities that held significant numbers of such detainees. Authorities continued to refuse to divulge information regarding numbers or names of persons detained on political or security-related charges. In October the VDC database of names and profiles of those detained since the beginning of the conflict contained more than 65,000 individuals. Authorities generally held them without charge or trial and did not inform their families. If authorities tried them, political detainees appeared in criminal courts for such charges. The government did not grant international organizations access to political prisoners.

Prison conditions for political or national security prisoners, especially accused opposition members, reportedly continued to be much worse than those for common criminals. According to local NGOs, authorities deliberately placed political prisoners in crowded cells with convicted and alleged felons and subjected them to verbal and physical threats and abuse. Political prisoners also reported they often slept on the ground due to lack of beds and faced frequent searches. According to reports from families, authorities refused many political prisoners access to family and counsel. Some former detainees and human rights observers reported the government denied political prisoners access to reading materials, including the Quran, and prohibited them from praying in their cells.

Many prominent civilian activists and journalists detained or forcibly disappeared following the 2011 protests reportedly remained in detention. There were no known developments in the many cases of reported disappearances from prior years, including the following persons believed forcibly disappeared by government forces: Abdel Aziz Kamal al-Rihawi; Alawite opposition figure Abdel Aziz al-Khair; Kurdish activist Berazani Karro; Yassin Ziadeh, brother of dissident Radwan Ziadeh; human rights lawyer Khalil Ma'touq and his assistant Mohamed Zaza; freedom of speech defender Bassel Khartabil; human rights activist Adel Barazi; peace activist and theater director Zaki Kordillo and his son Mihyar Kordillo.

There were no updates in the kidnappings of the following persons believed to have been abducted by Da'esh, armed opposition, or unidentified armed groups: activists Razan Zaitouneh, Wael Hamada, Samira Khalil, and Nazim Hamadi; religious leaders Bolous Yazigi and Yohanna Ibrahim; and peace activist Paulo Dall'Oglio. These individuals were among the estimated thousands of disappearances reported by activists and media.

HRW reported that courts continued to detain activists under the Counterterrorism Law implemented following the lifting of the Emergency Law in 2011. The government established the CTC under the Ministry of Justice to apply the law. Authorities held some detainees under this law at Adra central prison in Damascus pending trial. The amnesties enacted in 2014 and 2015 included some detainees held under counterterrorism charges, but NGOs and activists reported that the government released very few such individuals under the amnesties. Authorities later rearrested many of those released.

Local NGOs reported Da'esh detained and harassed domestic human rights activists, humanitarian aid workers, and religious figures. The COI reported that in Raqqa governorate Da'esh detained hundreds of prisoners, including women and community activists, who opposed its rule.

Civil Judicial Procedures and Remedies

Government civil remedies for human rights violations were functionally nonexistent. In areas under their control, opposition groups had not organized consistent civil judicial procedures. Da'esh and other extremist groups had no known civil judicial mechanisms in the territories they controlled.

Property Restitution

Security forces routinely seized detainees' property and personal items. With the onset of civil unrest, authorities increased confiscation of personal telephones, computers, and electronics. Security forces did not catalog these items in accordance with the law, and although detained individuals had the right to retrieve their confiscated belongings after release, authorities often did not return the property. According to media reports and activists, government forces also seized property left by refugees or internally displaced persons.

According to humanitarian aid workers, Da'esh seized property from international and local aid workers at checkpoints that Da'esh controlled throughout the country.

f. Arbitrary or Unlawful Interference with Privacy, Family, Home, or Correspondence

The law prohibits such actions, but they occurred routinely. Police frequently bypassed search warrant requirements in criminal cases by citing security reasons or emergency grounds for entry into private property. Random home raids occurred in large cities and towns of most governorates where the government maintained a presence, usually following large antigovernment protests or opposition attacks against government targets.

The government continued to open mail addressed to both citizens and foreign residents and routinely monitored internet communications, including e-mail (see section 2.a.).

The government continued to bar membership in some political organizations, including Islamist parties, and often arrested their members (see section 3).

g. Abuses in Internal Conflict

The government, opposition groups, and Da'esh escalated their use of force during the year. The Office of the UN High Commissioner for Human Rights (OHCHR) reported that more than 250,000 persons had died since the start of protests in 2011, but OHCHR stopped recording this statistic in 2014. In April the UN special envoy for Syria estimated that the fighting had resulted in the deaths of more than 400,000 persons since 2011. In January media outlets widely reported that the government used "surrender or starve" tactics in hard-to-reach and besieged areas of the country. Soldiers surrounding besieged areas set up checkpoints to profit from the limited supply of goods, prices for which rose multiple times in besieged areas. The UN also reported that rebel groups imposed a siege on the villages of Fuah and Kefraya in Idlib province. The SNHR reported that Russian airstrikes on Hama, Homs, Idlib, Aleppo, Latakia, and Raqqa governorates killed 3,967 civilians throughout the year.

Government forces, Da'esh, and opposition forces attacked civilian institutions, including schools, hospitals, religious establishments, and bakeries. The SNHR noted 45 percent of the country's hospitals were not functioning due to government shelling and looting, and in many opposition-held areas even fewer hospitals functioned.

<u>Killings</u>: The government reportedly committed the majority of killings throughout the year (see section 1.a.).

Government killings and use of lethal tactics reportedly increased during the year, despite a brief decrease during early March at the start of the period designated by the Cessation of Hostilities statement. The SNHR reported the government was responsible for the deaths of 6,924 civilians from January through November and Da'esh killed 1,397 civilians during the same period.

Reports from NGOs, including reports cited by the United Nations indicated that summary killings of civilians took place in the city of Aleppo in December as government forces retook opposition-held areas. These reports also indicated that government and allied forces targeted members of first-responder groups and that men between the ages of 30 and 50 were either detained by the government or immediately conscripted into the army. Reports cited by the United Nations also indicated that armed rebel groups prevented some civilians from escaping.

Progovernment militias reportedly continued to carry out mass killings. According to the SNHR, government-affiliated sectarian militias perpetrated massacres in the cities of Homs and Aleppo. In a June 2015 report on ethnic massacres, the SNHR noted that in February 2015 sectarian militia raided homes in the as-Sabil neighborhood of Homs, killing 14 civilians, including four children and five women. Additionally, in February 2015 Shiite militia reportedly kidnapped 320 individuals from two Aleppo villages and used them as human shields while retreating; fighting in this incident killed 48 civilians.

Opposition forces reportedly increased their killing of government forces, suspected government supporters, and members of minority communities through large-scale attacks and the use of snipers. According to the COI, opposition forces positioned military facilities and equipment in civilian areas. In 2012 several opposition commanders reportedly drafted and endorsed codes of conduct in an effort to curb violations and killings. Adherence to such standards was uneven. Media reports and videos from the country reported the deliberate killing by Da'esh and opposition forces of unarmed prisoners, including government soldiers. In some cases informal courts reportedly tried prisoners in an irregular fashion, such as facing a sharia council prior to execution, according to reports from international NGOs and the COI.

Extremist groups operating in spaces vacated by government forces also committed a large number of abuses and violations. There were unconfirmed reports that Da'esh executed tens of Arab and Kurdish civilians on March 21 before fleeing Kafr Saghir as government forces seized the area. According to the COI, Da'esh directed multiple bombings of medical centers in areas seized by the Kurdish People's Protection Units (YPG) and targeted civilians with suicide bombings in streets full of civilians and near hospitals.

Other Syrian armed groups engaged in abuses. According to the COI, Jabhat al-Nusra killed more than 20 Druze in a massacre in Idlib governorate in June 2015. The SNHR attributed 132 civilian deaths to the PYD and other Kurdish groups.

Abductions: The government was reportedly responsible for the majority of disappearances during the year. Armed extremist groups not affiliated with the government also reportedly kidnapped individuals, particularly in the northern areas, targeting religious leaders, aid workers, suspected government affiliates, journalists, and activists. In August the SNHR attributed approximately 96 percent (nearly 72,000) of the estimated 75,000 forced disappearances to the government. The SNHR attributed 1,479 disappearances to Da'esh, 892 to al-Nusra Front, 397 to the PYD and other Kurdish forces, and 306 to armed opposition forces.

According to reliable NGO reports, government forces as well as Da'esh routinely kidnapped and detained aid providers and severely restricted humanitarian access to territories under their respective control. Activists reported aid workers in Da'esh-controlled territory were at high risk of abduction or violence.

In 2014 Da'esh reportedly abducted thousands of Yezidi women from Iraq and brought them to Syria for sale in markets or as rewards for Da'esh fighters. Fighters held the women as slaves and subjected them and other captured women and girls to repeated sexual violence, systematic rape, forced marriages, and coerced abortions. In interviews with the COI, they described multiple rapes by several men, including incidents of gang rape. Numerous NGOs and activists also reported that Da'esh fighters raped women in Da'esh-held areas or forced them to marry Da'esh fighters. Towards the end of the year, most of the abducted girls and women remained in Da'esh custody.

In June the COI issued a report called "They Came to Destroy: ISIS Crimes Against the Yazedis" that concluded "ISIS has committed the crime of genocide as well as multiple crimes against humanity and war crimes against the Yezidis, thousands of whom are held captive in the Syrian Arab Republic where they are subjected to almost unimaginable horrors."

The location and status of Khalil Arfu and Sukfan Amin Hamza from Derek, Hasakah governorate, and members of the Kurdistan Democratic Party remained unknown.

The COI reported that a dramatic rise in hostage taking, which was often sectarian in nature, triggered reprisals and fueled intercommunal tension. Opposition armed groups abducted civilians and members of government forces to enable prisoner exchanges and for ransom money to purchase weapons.

<u>Physical Abuse, Punishment, and Torture</u>: According to reliable NGO reports, the government and its affiliated militias consistently engaged in physical abuse, punishment, and torture of both opposition members and civilians. Government agents targeted individuals with previous ties to foreign governments that favored the opposition; it also targeted family members and associates of such individuals. Government officials reportedly abused prisoners and detainees, as well as injured and sick persons, and raped women and men as a tactic of war. Additionally, according to the COI, the "Caesar photographs" smuggled out of the country in 2014 by a former government photographer documented the torture and severe malnourishment of more than 11,000 deceased detainees between 2011 and 2013.

The SNHR reported that authorities forced prisoners to witness the rape of other prisoners, threatened them with the rape of family members (in particular female family members), forced them to undress, and insulted their beliefs. According to the COI, the government and affiliated militias systematically perpetrated rape and other attacks on civilian populations in Deir al-Zour, Dara'a, Hama, Damascus, and Tartus governorates. Detention centers were the most common location for reported abuse, but attacks also occurred during military raids and at checkpoints. Reports included instances in which multiple attackers, usually soldiers and shabiha, gang-raped women in their homes, sometimes in front of family members. Observers believed sexual violence was widespread and underreported. In 2015 the SNHR estimated government forces were responsible for at least 7,672 incidents of sexual abuse since the beginning of the conflict. The SNHR noted an increased use of sexual violence against women before granting permission to depart besieged areas or to return with medical supplies and food.

There were widespread reports that Da'esh also engaged in abuses and brutality. According to the COI, Da'esh increased brutal treatment of those it captured in Raqqa, Deir al-Zour, and Aleppo governorates. Da'esh frequently punished victims publicly and forced residents, including children, to watch executions and amputations. Activists, NGOs, and the media reported numerous accounts of women in Da'esh-held territory facing arbitrary and severe punishments, including execution by stoning. Da'esh also committed abuses systematically against captured Free Syrian Army (FSA) and YPG fighters. Da'esh fighters reportedly beat captives (including with cables) during interrogations and killed those held in its detention centers in Raqqa and Aleppo governorates. Da'esh also beat persons because of their dress; several sources reported Da'esh members beat women for not covering their faces. Da'esh justified its use of corporal punishment, including amputations and lashings, under religious law.

The COI also reported in previous years that armed groups, under the banner of the FSA, tortured and executed suspected government agents, members of the shabiha, and collaborators. The COI noted that some opposition groups subjected detainees suspected of being members of pro-government militias to severe physical or mental pain and suffering to obtain information or confessions, or as punishment or coercion. The report also noted instances in which extremist groups Jabhat al-Nusra and Da'esh arbitrarily detained and tortured individuals passing through checkpoints along the country's northern border.

<u>Child Soldiers</u>: Several sources documented the continued recruitment and use of children in combat. The COI reported that pro-government militias enlisted children as young as 13. The COI reported the government sometimes paid children between the ages of six and 13 to be informants, exposing them to danger. There were no new reports during the year of combatants recruiting boys between the ages of 12 and 14 to conduct surveillance in Aleppo governorate. In the earlier years of the conflict, most of the children recruited by armed forces and groups were boys between 15 and 17 years old and served primarily in support roles away from the front lines. Since 2014, however, all parties to the conflict recruited children at much younger ages--as young as seven years old--and often without parental consent.

More than half of the UN Children's Fund (UNICEF)-verified cases of children recruited in 2015 were under 15 years old, compared with less than 20 percent in 2014. These children received military training, participated in combat or took up life-threatening roles in combat zones, including carrying and maintaining weapons, manning checkpoints, and treating and evacuating war wounded. Parties to the conflict used children to kill, including as executioners or snipers.

HRW reported opposition forces used children under the age of 18 as fighters. According to HRW, numerous groups and factions failed to prevent the enlistment of minors, while Da'esh and Jabhat al-Nusra actively recruited children as fighters. According to the COI, Islamic Front-affiliated and other armed groups "recruited, trained, and used children in active combat roles." Jaish al-Mujaheddin enlisted minors younger than 18, according to the COI. A Da'esh camp near Aleppo trained children as young as 14. In Raqqa governorate, according to the COI, Da'esh recruited and enlisted children as young as 10. HRW noted that Ahrar al-Sham, Jabhat al-Nusra, and YPG militias enlisted fighters under the age of 18.

The COI report also confirmed that the YPG demobilized child soldiers from its ranks and began monitoring adherence to its commitment to eliminate children from fighting. Nevertheless, some local groups reported YPG and Asayish forces abused and forcibly recruited children.

The Institute for War and Peace Reporting noted that activists in Idlib governorate launched a campaign to prevent the recruitment of child soldiers.

Also see the Department of State's annual *Trafficking in Persons Report* at www.state.gov/j/tip/rls/tiprpt/.

<u>Other Conflict-related Abuses</u>: Both the government and opposition forces impeded the flow of humanitarian assistance. According to the UN Office for Humanitarian Assistance (OCHA), by October more than 861,000 civilians resided in besieged areas impossible to access. The COI reported that government forces, opposition forces, and Da'esh all employed sieges to devastating effects, deliberately restricting the passage of relief supplies and access by humanitarian agencies. Government forces were responsible for the majority of such activity. Acute restrictions on food and medicine reportedly caused malnutrition-related deaths, as well as outbreaks of hepatitis, cutaneous leishmaniasis, typhoid, and dysentery. While the country's malnutrition rates largely remained below emergency thresholds during the year, the United Nations recorded pockets of malnutrition, primarily in besieged areas. The COI reported that government forces continued to besiege rebel-held areas in southern and eastern Damascus to render the conditions of life unbearable and force civilians to flee. In areas where combatants reached local truces, such as Moadimiyeh, civilians continued to suffer from shortages of food and medicine. From 2012 until June, the government denied UN-facilitated food and medicine intended for four thousand besieged residents in Darayya. The Damascus suburb surrendered to government forces in August.

In September, UNICEF reported emaciated children and a rise in the rates of caesarean sections and miscarriages, due to a shortage of food and medicine in Madaya, a besieged area. The government also failed to provide visas to international humanitarian workers and created unnecessary bureaucratic obstacles to relief delivery. The COI and the media reported that opposition groups also surrounded towns and limited access to supplies such as food in Afrin, Nubl, Zahra, and other locations. Da'esh imposed a siege of government-controlled areas of Deir al-Zour governorate.

The COI found that the government detained many Red Crescent volunteers and medical staff on the pretext of "having supported terrorists." According to reliable NGO reports, the government's continued bombardment, which they characterized as indiscriminate, destroyed and damaged health-care facilities in opposition-held areas, such as the Hama governorate and Aleppo city. On September 19, aircraft bombed a SARC-escorted UN convoy traveling to Orem al-Kubra in rural Aleppo, killing more than 20 civilians and aid workers. A UN investigative panel concluded in December that it was highly likely that the attack was perpetrated by the Syrian Arab Air Force.

According to the COI, the Islamic Front and Jaish al-Mujaheddin stopped or limited electricity and water to several neighborhoods in Aleppo.

Observers and international aid organizations reported that the government specifically targeted health-care workers, medical facilities, ambulances, and patients and restricted access to medical facilities and services to civilians and prisoners, particularly in Aleppo City. The COI also reported that government sniper fire and military assaults on medical facilities intentionally targeted sick and injured persons as well as pregnant women and persons with disabilities. According to credible NGO and COI reports, the government deliberately obstructed the efforts of sick and injured persons to obtain help, and many such individuals elected not to seek medical assistance in hospitals due to fear of arrest, detention, torture, or death. Government forces also reportedly targeted medical professionals for arrest. Physicians for Human Rights (PHR) released a report in July stating that 269 medical facilities sustained 382 attacks between 2011 and June. PHR reported that the government and its allies committed 90 percent of these attacks. PHR reported that 757 medical personnel were killed between 2011 and June, the majority by the government and its allies.

In October Russian forces in support of the government dropped cluster bombs on M10, the largest opposition-supported hospital in eastern Aleppo City. It had already suffered heavy bombardment three days earlier, in an assault UN Secretary-General Ban Ki-moon denounced as a war crime.

Government and opposition forces reportedly used civilians, including women and children, to shield combatants.

All participants in the conflict used provocative sectarian rhetoric, which the COI warned risked inciting mass indiscriminate violence. According to the COI, the rise in government-supported militias composed mostly of religious minorities and the positioning of these militias within their respective supportive communities fostered sectarian hostilities.

The COI noted mass displacements of communities under Da'esh control, where Da'esh officials warned residents to conform to Da'esh standards or leave. Communities experienced discriminatory sanctions, including specialized religious taxes ("jizya"), forced religious conversions, destruction of religious sites, and expulsion of minority communities. In January the SNHR reported that YPG forces forcibly displaced Arab residents in areas liberated by Kurdish forces. When the YPG-affiliated Syrian Democratic Forces began moving to liberate areas from Da'esh in August, human rights groups and humanitarian actors reported that the forces established local governing bodies not representative of or credible with local communities and hindered the work of independent civil society and humanitarian organizations.

International media reported widely on government and nongovernment forces attacking and destroying religious as well as UNESCO world heritage sites. The American Academy for the Advancement of Science (AAAS) noted many instances of visible damage to cultural heritage sites. In Aleppo the AAAS found massive destruction throughout the city, especially within the World Heritage site of the ancient city. According to weekly incident reports from the American Schools of Oriental Research, government forces continued to target mosques and churches. Government forces also pillaged and destroyed property, including homes, farms, and businesses of defectors and opposition figures.

Section 2. Respect for Civil Liberties, Including:

a. Freedom of Speech and Press

While the constitution provides for freedom of speech and press, the government severely restricted these rights, often terrorizing, abusing, or killing those who attempted to exercise these rights.

<u>Freedom of Speech and Expression</u>: The government routinely characterized expression as illegal, and individuals could not criticize the government publicly or privately without fear of reprisal. The government also stifled criticism by invoking penal code articles prohibiting acts or speech inciting sectarianism. It monitored political meetings and relied on informer networks.

<u>Press and Media Freedoms</u>: The government continued to exercise extensive control over local print and broadcast media, and the law imposes strict punishment for reporters who do not reveal their government sources in response to government requests. A number of quasi-independent periodicals, usually owned and produced by individuals with government connections, published during the year. In 2014 the government began allowing very limited use of Kurdish in state-run universities, following a decades-long, mostly ineffective ban prohibiting all Kurdish-language publications (see section 6, National/Racial/Ethnic Minorities).

The government owned some radio and most local television companies, and the Ministry of Information closely monitored all radio and television news and entertainment programs for adherence to government policies. Despite restrictions on ownership and use, citizens widely used satellite dishes, although the government jammed some Arab networks.

Books critical of the government were illegal.

Extremist organizations such as Jabhat al-Nusra, Jund al-Aqsa, and Da'esh also posed a serious threat to press and media freedoms.

<u>Violence and Harassment</u>: Government forces reportedly detained, arrested, and harassed journalists and other writers for works deemed critical of the state. Harassment included attempts at intimidation, banning such individuals from the country, dismissing journalists from their positions, and ignoring requests for continued accreditation. According to reliable NGO reports, the government routinely arrested journalists who were either associated with or writing in favor of the political opposition or the FSA and instigated attacks against foreign press outlets throughout the country.

The government and Da'esh routinely targeted and killed both local and foreign journalists, according to the COI. According to Freedom on the Net and the Committee to Protect Journalists (CPJ), Syria remained the most deadly and dangerous country in the world for journalists. During the year the CPJ documented the deaths of three journalists in the country: Khaled al-Iissa, Osama Jumaa, and Majid Dirani. According to the CPJ, the majority of reporters killed were covering politics and human rights issues. Reporters Without Borders (RSF) estimated 56 journalists were killed between 2011 and September, including seven during the year.

A June 16 attack in Aleppo City injured prominent Syrian activist Hadi al-Abdullah and killed photographer Khaled al-Issa, both affiliated with the popular opposition media outlet Radio Fresh. No group took responsibility for the attack; however, it signified the risks to activists and journalists affiliated with opposition groups.

According to the RSF, eight journalists and 17 netizens (activists who may not have journalist training but who use the internet to disseminate their work) remained in prison. The CPJ reported that seven journalists remained in government detention. The reason for arrests was often unclear. Arbitrary arrest raised fears that authorities could arrest internet users at any time for simple online activities perceived to threaten the government's control, such as posting on a blog, tweeting, commenting on Facebook, sharing a photograph, or uploading a video.

According to reports from media outlets operating in areas controlled by the PYD, they faced pressure and received online threats demanding they play pro-PYD songs. Reports indicated that some opposition journalists affiliated with the Kurdish National Council were detained and/or beaten by members of the PYD security services. In May an independent radio station in al Hasakah governorate reported that an anonymous armed group attacked its headquarters, set the building on fire, and threatened to kill the head of the station if he did not stop broadcasting. Following the attack many local and international governments and political parties criticized the attack, including the Executive Authority of the Self-Administration in the area.

Censorship or Content Restrictions: The government continued to control the dissemination of information strictly, including developments regarding fighting between the government and armed opposition, and prohibited most criticism of the government and discussion of sectarian problems, including religious and ethnic minority rights. The Ministries of Information and Culture censored domestic and foreign publications prior to circulation or importation and prevented circulation of content determined critical or sensitive. The government prohibited publication or distribution of any material security officials deemed threatening or embarrassing to the government. Censorship was usually greater for materials in Arabic.

Local journalists reported they engaged in extensive self-censorship on subjects such as criticism of the president and his family, the security services, or Alawite religious groups. The government required both domestic and foreign journalist who did not observe these guidelines to leave the country or targeted them for arrest, torture, or execution.

Libel/Slander Laws: Although the 2011 media law prohibits imprisoning journalists for practicing their profession, the government continued to detain and arrest journalists who opposed the government. The government charged some of these individuals under libel laws.

National Security: The government cited laws protecting national security to restrict media distribution of material that criticized government policies or public officials.

<u>Nongovernmental Impact</u>: Opposition forces kidnapped and killed journalists. According to the RSF and SNHR, the PYD subjected journalists to harassment and detention. According to the COI, Da'esh abducted journalists and activists working to document its abuses in territories under its control. According to the SNHR Da'esh killed 14 media activists including a woman and held others in detention. The SNHR also reported that opposition groups killed six media activists and injured two, and it alleged that Russian forces killed six.

Internet Freedom

According to the 2016 *Freedom on the Net Report*, the country remained one of the most dangerous and repressive environments for internet users in the world. The government controlled and restricted the internet and monitored e-mail and social media accounts. Individuals and groups could not express views via the internet, including by e-mail, without prospect of reprisal. The government applied the media law, as well as the general legal code, to regulate internet use and prosecute users.

The government often monitored internet communications, including e-mail, and interfered with and blocked internet service, SMS messages, and two-step verification messages for password recovery or account activation. The government employed sophisticated technologies and hundreds of computer specialists for filtering and surveillance purposes, such as monitoring e-mail and social media accounts of detainees, activists, and others. The government did not attempt to restrict the security branches' monitoring and censoring of the internet. The security branches were largely responsible for restricting internet freedom and access; internet blackouts often coincided with security force attacks. The government censored websites related to the opposition, including the websites for local coordination committees as well as media outlets.

Many areas no longer had internet access because of continued violence and damage to infrastructure largely perpetrated by the government, especially in the north and east. The government also restricted or prohibited internet access in areas under siege. It obstructed connectivity through its control of key infrastructure, at times shutting the internet and mobile telephone networks entirely or at particular sites of unrest. There was generally little access to state-run internet service in besieged areas unless users could capture signals clandestinely from rooftops near government-controlled areas. Some towns in opposition-held areas had limited internet access via satellite connections. Some activists reportedly gained access independently to satellite internet or through second and third-generation (3G) cell phone network coverage.

The government meanwhile expanded its efforts to use social media, such as Instagram, Twitter, and Facebook, to spread pro-government propaganda and manipulate online content. Government authorities routinely tortured and beat journalists to extract passwords for social media sites, and the Syrian Electronic Army (SEA), a group of pro-government computer hackers, frequently launched cyberattacks on websites to disable them and post pro-government material. In January authorities detained Abdul Moyeen Hommse, a media activist, for posting a video satirizing Asad's government. Later he lost his job. In addition to promoting hacking and conducting surveillance, the government and groups that it supported, such as the SEA, reportedly planted malware to target human rights activists, opposition members, and journalists. Local human rights groups blamed government personnel for instances in which malware infected activists' computers.

Observers also accused the SEA of slowing internet access to force self-censorship on government critics and diverting e-mail traffic to government servers for surveillance.

Da'esh forces restricted access to internet cafes, especially for women, confiscated cell phones and computers, and instituted strict rules for journalists to follow or face punishment. In February, Da'esh banned private internet access and closed all internet cafes across Manbij, a city in northern Aleppo governorate. Da'esh also increased cyberattacks on journalists and groups documenting human rights abuses. In April Da'esh killed journalist Mohammed Zahir al-Sherqat in response to al-Sherqat's activism.

Academic Freedom and Cultural Events

The government restricted academic freedom and cultural events. Authorities generally did not permit teachers to express ideas contrary to government policy. The Ministry of Culture restricted and banned the screening of certain films.

Da'esh and Jabhat al-Nusra sought to restrict academic freedom severely and to curtail cultural events considered un-Islamic. Media sources reported that schools in Da'esh-controlled Raqqa governorate banned several academic subjects, including chemistry and philosophy.

During the year students, particularly those residing in opposition-held areas, continued to face challenges in taking nationwide exams. The government, however, allowed 360 students from Moadimiyeh and 68 students from Madaya to travel to government-held areas to take exams in May.

b. Freedom of Peaceful Assembly and Association

Freedom of Assembly

The constitution provides for the right of assembly, but the government restricted this right. Even after the 2011 repeal of the emergency law, a subsequent 2011 presidential decree grants the government broad powers over freedom of assembly.

The Ministry of Interior requires permission for demonstrations or any public gathering of more than three persons. As a rule the ministry authorized only demonstrations by the government, affiliated groups, or the Baath Party, orchestrating them on numerous occasions. The government continued to use excessive force against peaceful demonstrators.

In opposition-held areas, extremist armed opposition groups targeted activists, protesters, documentation groups, and media groups for detention, hostage taking, harassment, and executions. The COI reported that residents in Da'esh-controlled parts of Aleppo and Raqqa governorates noted severe restrictions on assembly.

According to allegations by Kurdish activists and in press reporting, the PYD and the YPG suppressed freedom of assembly and severely limited freedom of speech in areas under their control.

Freedom of Association

The constitution permits private associations but grants the government the right to limit their activities. The government restricted freedom of association, requiring prior registration and approval for private associations and restricting the activities of associations and their members. The executive boards of professional associations were not independent of the government.

The government often denied requests for registration or failed to act on them, reportedly on political grounds. None of the local human rights organizations operated with a license, but many functioned under organizations that had requisite government registration. The government continued to block the multi-year effort by journalists to form a countrywide media association. The government selectively enforced the 2011 decree allowing the establishment of independent political parties, allowing only progovernment groups to form official parties (see section 3). According to local human rights groups, opposition activists declined to organize parties, fearing the government would use party lists to target opposition members.

Under the authority of laws that criminalize membership and activity in illegal organizations as determined by the government, security forces detained hundreds of persons linked to local human rights groups and prodemocracy student groups. The government also searched these individuals' personal and social media contacts for further potential targets.

According to media reports and reports from former residents of Da'esh-controlled areas, Da'esh did not permit the existence of associations that opposed the structures or policies of the "caliphate."

c. Freedom of Religion

See the Department of State's *International Religious Freedom Report* at www.state.gov/religiousfreedomreport/.

d. Freedom of Movement, Internally Displaced Persons, Protection of Refugees, and Stateless Persons

The constitution provides for freedom of movement "within the territories of the state unless restricted by a judicial decision or by the implementation of laws." The government, Da'esh, and other armed groups, however, restricted internal movement and travel and instituted security checkpoints to monitor such travel throughout the regions under their respective control. Government sieges in Homs, Damascus, Rif-Damascus, Deir al-Zour, and Idlib governorates resulted in documented cases of death, starvation, and severe malnutrition (see section 1.g.). Opposition forces imposed sieges on government-held areas in Aleppo governorate, cutting off water, electricity, fuel, and medicine. In areas under its control, Da'esh restricted the movement of government supporters or assumed supporters, especially the Alawi and Shia populations. Other opponents of the government also restricted the movement of such individuals, but to a lesser extent.

<u>Abuse of Migrants, Refugees, and Stateless Persons</u>: Both government and opposition forces reportedly besieged, shelled, and otherwise made practically

inaccessible some Palestinian refugee camps, neighborhoods, and sites, which resulted in severe malnutrition, lack of access to medical care and humanitarian assistance, and civilian deaths.

In-country Movement: In government-besieged cities throughout the country, government forces blocked humanitarian access, leading to severe malnutrition, lack of access to medical care, and death, particularly in the cities of Zabadani, Douma, and Eastern Ghouta (see section 1.g.). According to OCHA, 590,000 persons remained in 18 besieged areas. The violence, coupled with significant cultural pressure, severely restricted the movement of women in many areas. Additionally, the law allows certain male relatives to place travel bans on women (see section 6, Women).

The government inconsistently cooperated with UNHCR and other humanitarian organizations in assisting internally displaced persons, refugees, and asylum seekers. The government provided some cooperation to the United Nations Relief and Works Agency for Palestinian Refugees in the Near East (UNRWA).

The government relied on security checkpoints to monitor and limit movement and expanded them into civilian areas. The government also barred foreign diplomats from visiting most parts of the country and rarely granted them permission to travel outside Damascus. The consistently high level and unpredictability of violence severely restricted movement throughout the country.

Da'esh and opposition groups also controlled movement, including with checkpoints.

Government forces reportedly used snipers to prevent protests, enforce curfews, target opposition forces, and in some cases to prevent civilians from fleeing besieged towns. According to the COI, the drive through long desert detour routes exposed passengers and drivers to arbitrary arrest, unlawful search and seizure of property, demands for bribes, and detention and execution at checkpoints administered by Da'esh, the government, and other armed actors.

Da'esh reportedly did not permit female passengers to traverse territory it controlled unless accompanied by a close male relative.

Foreign Travel: While citizens have the right to travel internationally, the government denied passports and other vital documents based on the applicant's political views, association with opposition groups, or ties to geographic areas where the opposition dominated. The government also imposed exit visa requirements and routinely closed the Damascus airport and border crossings, claiming the closures were due to violence or threats of violence. Additionally, the government often banned travel by human rights or civil society activists, their families, and affiliates. Many citizens reportedly learned of the ban against their travel only when authorities prevented them from departing the country. The government reportedly applied travel bans without explanation or explicit duration, including in cases when individuals sought to travel for health reasons. The government comprehensively banned international travel of opposition members, often targeting any such individual who attempted to travel. Local media and human rights groups repeatedly stated that opposition activists and their families hesitated to leave the country, fearing attacks at airports and border crossings. In June, Turkish border guards killed 11 Syrian refugees when they attempted to flee from the country.

There were reports Da'esh destroyed Syrian passports and legal records and produced its own passports, not recognized by any country or entity. These policies disproportionately affected children, because many left the country before obtaining a passport or identification card. Additionally, Syrians born abroad to parents who fled the conflict and remained in refugee camps generally did not have access to Syrian citizenship documents. The government in 2015 began allowing Syrians living outside of the country whose passports expired to renew their passports at consulates. Many who fled as refugees, however, feared reporting to the government against which they may have protested or feared the government could direct reprisals against family members still in the country.

Women over 18 have the legal right to travel without the permission of male relatives, but a husband may file a request with the Interior Ministry to prohibit his wife from departing the country.

Da'esh explicitly prohibited women from foreign travel.

<u>Emigration and Repatriation</u>: On their return to the country, both persons who unsuccessfully sought asylum in other countries and those who had previous connections with the Syrian Muslim Brotherhood faced prosecution. The law provides for the prosecution of any person who attempts to seek refuge in another country to evade penalty in Syria. The government routinely arrested dissidents and former citizens with no known political affiliation who attempted to return to the country after years or even decades of self-imposed exile. Many emigrants who did not complete mandatory military service could pay a fee to avoid

conscription while visiting the country, but this option tended to vary by ethnicity and socioeconomic status. Authorities exempted from military service without payment persons of Syrian origin born in a foreign country but able to demonstrate service in the army of the country of birth.

Internally Displaced Persons

The government largely did not facilitate humanitarian assistance for IDPs and provided inconsistent protection. During the year violence continued to be the primary reason for citizens to leave the country, much of the violence attributed to government and Russian aerial attacks. Years of conflict repeatedly displaced persons; each displacement depleted family assets and eroded coping mechanisms.

By the last quarter of the year, the United Nations estimated there were more than 6.1 million IDPs in the country. The government generally did not provide sustainable access for services to the IDP population and did not offer IDPs assistance or protection. UN humanitarian officials reported that most IDPs sought shelter with host communities or in collective centers, abandoned buildings, or informal camps. In the first half of the year, intensified fighting in the governorates of Aleppo and al-Hasakah displaced more than 900,000 citizens. In September fighting displaced an additional 100,000 persons in Hama governorate. Observers estimated that 75,000 to 100,000 persons, displaced from all parts of the country, remained stranded at the border with Jordan in a location known as "the berm."

The SARC functioned as the main partner for international humanitarian organizations working inside the country to provide humanitarian assistance in both government- and opposition-controlled areas. Access difficulties--including those imposed by the government, Da'esh, and opposition groups--hindered the delivery of aid to persons in need. NGOs operating from Damascus faced extensive bureaucratic obstruction when attempting to provide relief to populations in need. The SARC and UN agencies sought to increase the flow of assistance to opposition-held areas to meet growing humanitarian needs. The government routinely disrupted the supply of humanitarian aid to rebel-held areas, particularly medical assistance (see section 1.g.).

The humanitarian response to the country was one of the largest in the world, coordinated through a complicated bureaucratic structure. The crisis inside the country continued to meet the UN criteria for a Level 3 response--the global humanitarian system's classification for response to the most severe, large-scale humanitarian crises. Cross-border operations from Turkey and Jordan provided humanitarian assistance for Syrians. Additional assistance came through cross-line operations originating from Damascus. Since the International Syria Support Group's Humanitarian Task Force began advocating for expanded access in February, the United Nations provided assistance to nearly 400,000 persons in 17 besieged areas, more than 817,000 in hard-to-reach locations, and 57,000 persons in priority cross-line areas, compared with 30,000 who received assistance in 2015. Assistance reached many besieged and hard-to-reach towns several times. Despite these efforts, however, the Asad government continued to hinder UN access, and many communities continued to suffer and surrender to the government's "starve and kneel" tactics.

OCHA reported that during July no humanitarian assistance reached more than four million persons in the country's hard-to-reach areas.

Protection of Refugees

Access to Asylum: The law provides for the granting of asylum or refugee status, and the government has established a system for providing protection to refugees. UNHCR and UNRWA were able to maintain limited protection areas for refugees and asylum seekers, although violence hampered access to vulnerable populations. In coordination with both local and international nongovernmental organizations, the United Nations continued to provide such individuals essential services and assistance.

UNHCR estimated that at least 95,000 persons, mainly Yezidi Iraqis, entered the country following Da'esh attacks on Sinjar District in Iraq, beginning in 2014. Many initially fled to Mount Sinjar but managed to evacuate the mountain with the assistance of military strikes led by the Western coalition and support from Syrian Kurdish groups, who transported many Yezidis into the country. The majority of these persons returned to Iraq through the Iraqi Kurdistan Region; however, in June UNHCR estimated there were approximately 10,000 Iraqis in camps in al-Hasakah governorate, including 2,262 Yezidis in the Newroz camp, 2,330 Sunni Arabs in Roj camp, and 5,700 in al-Hol camp. There were also some Iraqis in the cities of Malkia, Qamishly, Amuda, and Derbasia.

Employment: The law does not explicitly grant refugees, except for Palestinians, the right to work. While the government rarely granted non-Palestinian refugees a work permit, many refugees found work in the informal sector as guards, construction workers, street vendors, and in other manual jobs.

<u>Access to Basic Services</u>: The law allows for the issuance of identity cards to Palestinian refugees and the same access to basic services provided to citizens. The government also allowed Iraqi refugees access to publicly available services, such as health care and education, but residency permits were available only to those refugees who entered Syria legally and possessed a valid passport, which did not include all refugees. The lack of access to residency permits issued by the Syrian authorities exposed refugees to risks of harassment and exploitation and severely affected their access to public services. The approximately 30,000 non-Palestinian refugees in the country faced growing protection risks, multiple displacements, tightened security procedures at checkpoints, and difficulty obtaining required residency permits, all of which resulted in restrictions on their freedom of movement. UNHCR reported a rise in sexual- and gender-based violence and child protection concerns among refugees, including child labor, school dropouts, and early marriages.

Stateless Persons

Approximately 190,000 Kurds in the country are not entitled to Syrian nationality under the law. The government considered the Kurds to be foreigners, which denied them access to services. Following the 1962 census, approximately 150,000 Kurds lost their citizenship. A legislative decree ordained the single-day census in 1962, and the government executed it unannounced with regard to the inhabitants of al-Hasakah governorate. Government justification for this measure was to identify Kurds who had entered the country since 1945. Anyone not registered for any reason or without all required paperwork became "foreign" from that day onward. In similar fashion authorities recorded anyone who refused to participate as "undocumented." Because of this loss of citizenship, these Kurds and their descendants lacked identity cards and could not access government services, including health care and education. They also faced social and economic discrimination. Stateless Kurds do not have the right to inherit or bequeath assets, and their lack of citizenship or identity documents restricted their travel to and from the country.

In 2011 President Asad issued a decree declaring that stateless Kurds in al-Hasakah governorate who were registered as "foreigners" could apply for citizenship. UNHCR reported that approximately 40,000 of these were still unable to obtain citizenship. Likewise, the decree did not extend to the approximately 160,000 "unregistered" stateless Kurds. The change from 150,000 to 160,000 reflected an approximate increase in population since the 1962 census.

Children derive citizenship solely from their father. Because women cannot confer nationality on their children, an unknown number of children whose fathers were missing or deceased due to the continuing conflict were at risk of statelessness. Mothers could not pass citizenship to children born outside the country, including in neighboring countries operating refugee camps.

Section 3. Freedom to Participate in the Political Process

Although the constitution provides the ability for citizens to choose their government periodically through free and fair elections conducted by secret ballot and based on universal and equal suffrage, citizens were not able to exercise that ability. Outcomes did not reflect the unimpeded or uncoerced will of the electorate because of the underlying circumstances of elections.

Elections and Political Participation

Recent Elections: In April the country held geographically limited parliamentary elections, the results of which citizens living outside government control rejected. In 2014 Bashar Asad, Hassan al-Nouri, and Maher Hajjar registered as candidates for the June presidential election administered in disparate areas of the country; the majority of citizens could not access polling places because of violence or displacement. The process, in which Asad received 88.7 percent of the vote, was neither free nor fair by international standards. Voters faced intimidation by security elements, and the government forcibly transported state employees in Damascus to polling centers, according to observers and the media. Media reports described low overall voter turnout, even among those living in relatively stable areas with access to polling stations. Authorities allowed only persons in government-controlled territory, certain refugee areas, and refugees who left the country after obtaining official permission to vote. According to a 2014 report of Human Rights First, Hizballah threatened Syrian refugees if they did not vote for Asad. Security forces increased security measures in Damascus and surrounding areas under government control to maximize voter turnout. Nonetheless, violence continued throughout the country, and some armed opposition groups fired missiles at government-controlled areas during the voting period.

In October the National Coalition for the Syrian Revolutionary and Opposition Forces held internal elections in Istanbul, resulting in the re-election of the Syrian Opposition Coalition President Anas al-Abdah.

<u>Political Parties and Political Participation</u>: The constitution provides that the Baath Party is the ruling party and assures that it has a majority in all government and popular associations, such as workers' and women's groups. The Baath-led National Progressive Front dominated the 250-member People's Council, holding 200 of the 250 parliament seats following the April election. The Baath Party and nine other smaller satellite political parties constituted the coalition National Progressive Front. A 2011 decree allows establishment of additional political parties, although it forbids those based on religion, tribal affiliation, or regional interests.

Membership in the Baath Party or close familial relations with a prominent party member or powerful government official assisted in economic, social, and educational advancement. Party or government connections made it easier to gain admission to better schools, access lucrative employment, and achieve greater advancement and power within the government, the military, and the security services. The government reserved certain prominent positions, such as provincial governorships, solely for Baath Party members.

The government showed little tolerance for other political parties. The government harassed parties such as the Communist Union Movement, the Communist Action Party, and the Arab Social Union, and it arrested their members. Police arrested members of Islamist parties. Reliable data on illegal political parties was unavailable.

<u>Participation of Women and Minorities</u>: No laws limit the participation of women and members of minorities in the political process, and women and minorities did so. Women and minorities generally participated in the political system without formal restriction, although significant cultural and social barriers largely excluded women from decision-making positions. The government formed after the 2014 election included three female members: Vice President Najah al-Attar, Minister of State for Environmental Affairs Nazira Serkis, and Minister of Social Affairs Rima al-Qadiri. In 2015, 12 percent of the members of parliament were women. There were Christian, Druze, and Kurdish members in parliament. Alawites, the ruling religious minority, held greater political power than other minorities in the cabinet as well as greater power than the majority Sunni sect in the cabinet.

Section 4. Corruption and Lack of Transparency in Government

Although the law provides criminal penalties for official corruption, the government did not implement the law effectively, and officials frequently engaged in corrupt practices with impunity. Corruption continued to be a pervasive problem in police forces, security services, migration management agencies, and throughout the government.

Corruption: Due to the lack of free press and of opposition access to instruments of government and the media, there was almost no detailed information about corruption, except petty corruption. There were reports of prison guards demanding bribes from prisoners and their visitors. Visiting family members who paid higher bribes enjoyed visits to detainees without police surveillance. The price of bribes continued to rise from previous years. Human rights lawyers and family members of detainees stated that government officials in courts and prisons solicited bribes for favorable decisions and provision of basic services. Traffic police officers regularly solicited bribes from drivers, and child laborers reported bribing police to avoid arrest.

Financial Disclosure: There are no public financial disclosure laws for public officials. The prime minister's Central Commission for Control and Inspection is the main administrative body responsible for coordinating and monitoring public-sector corruption. Each government body, including the ministries, has a Control and Inspection Department that reported directly to the Central Commission.

Public Access to Information: The media law provides for access to information from ministries and other government institutions. The law contains ambiguous provisions for nondisclosure, including forbidding access to information that "affects national unity and national security." The law obliges authorities to respond to requests within seven days of receiving an inquiry. The law requires administrative judiciary courts to investigate total or partial refusals of information requests and issue a decision within one month. It does not stipulate penalties for noncompliance. There was no evidence the government implemented the law during the year.

Section 5. Governmental Attitude Regarding International and Nongovernmental Investigation of Alleged Violations of Human Rights

The government restricted attempts to investigate alleged human rights violations and actively refused to cooperate with any independent attempts to investigate alleged violations. The government did not grant permission for the formation of any domestic human rights organizations. Nevertheless, hundreds of such groups operated illegally in the country. There were reports the government harassed domestic human rights activists by subjecting them to regular surveillance and travel bans. The government normally responded to queries from human rights organizations and foreign embassies regarding specific cases by reporting that the case was still under investigation, that the prisoner in question had violated national security laws, or, if the case was in criminal court, that the executive branch could not interfere with the allegedly independent judiciary. The government reportedly sought out members of domestic human rights organizations for property seizures, harassment, detention, arrest, torture, and execution.

The government was highly suspicious of international human rights NGOs and did not allow them into the country. Reports and media interviews with government officials indicated the government denied committing any human rights violations. It denied other organizations access to several locations where government agents launched assaults on antigovernment protesters or allegedly held prisoners detained on political grounds. According to reliable reports, the government also actively restricted the activities of humanitarian aid organizations, especially along supply routes and access points near opposition-controlled areas (see section 1.g.).

The United Nations or Other International Bodies: The government continued to deny access to the UN Commission of Inquiry, mandated by the UN Human Rights Council to document and report on human rights violations and abuses in the country. It did not cooperate fully with numerous UN bodies, resulting in restrictions on access for humanitarian organizations, especially to opposition-controlled areas.

In its August 21 report, the Organization for the Prohibition of Chemical Weapons-United Nations Joint Investigative Mechanism (established to attribute responsibility for already-confirmed chemical warfare incidents) determined responsibility at a "sufficient" level for three of the nine attacks it reviewed. These attacks were a mustard gas attack by Da'esh in Marea, Aleppo governorate (August 2015), and two instances of chlorine used as a weapon by the government, specifically the Syrian Arab Air Force, in Talmenes, Idlib governorate (April 2014), and Sarmin, Idlib governorate (March 2015). A report from the Joint Investigative Mechanism in October found that the government used weaponized chlorine in 2015 in Qmenas as well.

Section 6. Discrimination, Societal Abuses, and Trafficking in Persons

Women

<u>Rape and Domestic Violence</u>: Rape is a felony, subject to punishment by at least 15 years in prison, but the government did not enforce the law. The law further stipulates that if the rapist marries the victim, the rapist receives no punishment. The victim's family sometimes agreed to this arrangement to avoid the social stigma attached to rape. There are no laws against spousal rape. Observers of the refugee crisis reported women, men, and community leaders consistently identified sexual violence as a primary reason their families fled the country. The COI reported rape was widespread, and government and progovernment forces used rape to terrorize and punish women, men, and children perceived as associated with the opposition (see section 1.g. for additional information, including on abuses committed by extremist groups). The COI concluded that underreporting and delayed reporting of sexual violence was endemic, rendering an assessment of its magnitude difficult. Reports by the SNHR, HRW, and other NGOs included interviews with female former prisoners, who reported that rape by guards and security forces was common in detention facilities.

The law does not specifically prohibit domestic violence, and violence against women was extensive and generally went unpunished. Victims did not report the vast majority of domestic violence and sexual assault cases. Victims traditionally were reluctant to seek assistance outside the family due to fear of social stigmatization. Security forces consistently treated violence against women as a social rather than a criminal matter. Observers reported that when some abused women tried to file a police report, police did not investigate their reports thoroughly, if at all, and that in other cases police officers responded by abusing the women, including by sexual harassment, verbal abuse, hair pulling, and slapping.

In the past several domestic violence centers operated in Damascus, and the government licensed and affiliated them with the Ministry of Social Affairs and Labor. Local NGOs reported, however, that many centers no longer operated due to the conflict. There were no known government-run services for women outside Damascus. According to local human rights organizations, local coordination committees and other opposition-related groups offered programming specifically for protection of women; NGOs did not integrate these programs throughout the country, and none reported reliable funding.

<u>Female Genital Mutilation/Cutting (FGM/C)</u>: There is no law against FGM/C; however, observers provided no reports of the abuse.

<u>Other Harmful Traditional Practices</u>: The law permits judges to reduce legal penalties for murder and assault if the defendant asserts an "honor" defense, which often occurred. The government kept no official statistics on use of this defense in murder and assault cases. There were no officially reported "honor" killings during the year, but local human rights groups asserted the practice continued, reportedly at previous levels, despite or even because of the continuing violence. NGOs working with refugees reported families killed some rape victims inside the country, including those raped by government forces, for reasons of "honor." NGOs also reported the conflict led to a significant rise in "honor" killings due to the pervasive use of rape by government forces and sexual slavery and exploitation by Da'esh.

<u>Sexual Harassment</u>: The law prohibits discrimination in employment on the basis of gender but does not explicitly prohibit sexual harassment. Due to social and cultural pressures, victims rarely reported sexual harassment.

<u>Reproductive Rights</u>: Couples and individuals have the right to decide freely the number, spacing, and timing of their children; manage their reproductive health; and generally have access to the information and means to do so, free from discrimination, coercion, or violence. Due to the conflict, there was limited access to reproductive health services, and restrictions on movement and lack of transportation affected the capacity of humanitarian response programs. The UN Population Fund (UNFPA) reported that infrastructure damage reduced the number of facilities and health personnel able to provide pregnant women with antenatal and postnatal care and skilled attendance at delivery. Activists also reported that government detention centers did not provide medical care to women during pregnancy or birth. Attacks on hospitals affected pregnant women, who were frequently unable to access care, and during the year observers reported to the Human Rights Council that hostilities forced an increasing number of women to give birth through caesarean sections to control the timing of their delivery and avoid traveling in insecure environments.

Female victims subjected to sexual violence lacked access to immediate health care. Consequences included severe physical injuries, psychosocial trauma, unwanted pregnancies, social stigmatization, and infection with sexually transmitted diseases, including HIV/AIDS. The destruction of hospitals further complicated access to health care. The lack of contraceptives caused many rape victims to face physical, social, and psychological consequences of both rape and any ensuing pregnancy.

Violence throughout the country made accessing medical care and reproductive services both costly and dangerous, and the COI reported that the government and armed extremists sometimes denied pregnant women passage through checkpoints, forcing them to give birth in unsterile and often dangerous conditions, without pain medication or adequate medical treatment. In February, UNFPA estimated that approximately 430,000 women in the country and in nearby refugee camps were pregnant and needed care. It also estimated that 70,000 would likely experience complications related to pregnancy or delivery. UNFPA provided reproductive health services to women by distributing reproductive health kits. According to numerous sources, government forces deliberately denied medical care to persons in areas controlled by the opposition.

Discrimination: Although the constitution provides for equality between men and women and the "right of every citizen to earn his wage according to the nature and yield of the work," the law does not explicitly stipulate equal pay for equal work. Moreover, a number of sections of family and criminal law do not treat men and women equally. Children derive citizenship solely from their father. An unknown number of children whose fathers were missing or deceased due to the continuing conflict were at risk of statelessness. Before the conflict began, only 16 percent of women participated in the formal labor force, compared with 72 percent of men. Female employment participation decreased as violence and insecurity increased. In previous years the government sought to overcome traditional discriminatory attitudes toward women and encouraged women's education by providing equal access to educational institutions, including universities.

The Commission for Family Affairs, Ministry of Justice, and Ministry of Social Affairs and Labor shared responsibility for attempting to afford equal legal rights to women. Governmental involvement in civil rights claims, including cases against sexual discrimination, was stagnant, and most claims went unanswered.

Personal status, retirement, citizenship, and social security laws discriminate against women. Men constituted the vast majority of the judiciary, and NGOs suggested this circumstance led to discriminatory treatment of women by federal courts. Under criminal law, if a man and a woman separately commit the same criminal act of adultery, the woman's punishment is double that of the man's. The law generally permits women to initiate divorce proceedings against their spouses, although some Christian sects strongly discouraged both women and men from doing so. For Muslims personal status law treats men and women differently. Some personal status laws mirror Islamic law regardless of the religion of those involved in the case. The law does not entitle a divorced woman to alimony in some cases, such as if she gave up her right to alimony to persuade her husband to agree to the divorce. Additionally, under the law a divorced mother loses the right to guardianship and physical custody of her sons when they reach age 13 and of her daughters at age 15, when guardianship transfers to the paternal side of the family.

The government's interpretation of Islamic law is the basis of inheritance law for all citizens except Christians. Accordingly, courts usually granted Muslim women half of the inheritance share of male heirs. In all communities male heirs must provide financial support to female relatives who inherit less. If they do not, women have the right to sue. During the year there were reports that in some regions custom prevailed over the law and women received no inheritance. A woman's husband, or male relative in a husband's absence, may request that the government prohibit his wife's travel abroad.

Women participated actively in public life and in most professions, including the armed forces, although violence in many regions reduced women's access to the public sphere. Women and men have equal legal rights in owning or managing land or other property, although cultural and religious norms impeded women's rights, especially in rural areas. Various sources observed that women constituted a minority of lawyers, university professors, and other professions. While women served in the judiciary, parliament, and high levels of government, the government often denied them decision-making positions (see section 3). According to several organizations, women were underrepresented in the judiciary, as only 13 percent of judges prior to the start of the civil war were women. The SNHR suggested that few, if any, women participated as judges in the courts.

Some opposition groups forbade women from participating equally in irregularly constituted courts (for example, in Aleppo governorate). Women did not hold an equal share of political positions in local opposition governance bodies but remained active in civil society, humanitarian assistance delivery, media, and education. Women did not have significant representation on local or provincial councils, according to NGOs.

Some opposition groups and extremist elements reportedly banned women from teaching and girls from attending school, particularly in Da'esh-controlled Deir al-Zour governorate. According to activists from Raqqa governorate, Da'esh segregated classrooms and removed women from the local councils in territories it controlled.

According to several groups, including HRW, extremist armed groups placed discriminatory restrictions on women and girls in Aleppo, al-Hasakah, Idlib, and Raqqa governorates. Such restrictions included strict dress codes, limitations on women's engagement in public life and ability to move freely, and constraints on their access to education and employment. Jabhat al-Nusra and Da'esh insisted that women follow a strict dress code that mandated wide cloaks and headscarves and that prohibited jeans, close-fitting clothing, and cosmetics. According to interviewees, members of these groups forbade women to appear in public without a male family member accompanying them in Idlib city, Ras al-Ayn, Tel Abyad (which was no longer in Da'esh control by year's end), and Tel Aran. Authorities threatened women and girls who did not abide by the restrictions with punishment and, in some cases, blocked them from using public transportation, accessing education, and buying bread. IDPs from the cities of Idlib, Tel Abyad, and Tel Aran related that Jabhat al-Nusra and Da'esh banned women from working outside the home.

In areas under its control, Da'esh published a "Civilization Document" with 16 points that a woman must follow or face the death penalty. They included staying at home and not leaving it without an immediate male relative (mahram); wearing a wide cloak, full face veil, and headscarf; closing hair salons; not sitting on chairs in public; and not seeing male doctors. Da'esh established the "al-Khanssaa" brigade, an all-female police force established in the city of Raqqa, composed mostly of noncitizen women who enforced these regulations, sometimes violently, among women.

There were limited reports of women actively participating in hostilities, including in armed Kurdish opposition groups and the mostly secular "Mother Aisha Brigade," considered part of the moderate armed opposition in the city of Aleppo. There also were limited reports of female Da'esh members actively participating in armed hostilities. In Raqqa Da'esh enlisted some women into the "al-Khanssaa" brigade, to staff checkpoints, enforce Da'esh laws, and participate in some house raids.

Children

Birth Registration: Children derive citizenship solely from their father. In large areas of the country where civil registries were not functioning, authorities did not register births. The government did not register the births of Kurdish noncitizen residents, including stateless Kurds (see section 2.d., Stateless Persons). Failure to register resulted in deprivation of services, such as diplomas for high school level studies, access to universities, access to formal employment, and civil documentation and protection.

Education: The government provided free public education to citizen children from primary school through university. Education is compulsory for all children between the ages of six and 12. Noncitizen children could also attend public schools at no cost but required permission from the Ministry of Education.

The conflict increasingly hampered the ability of children to attend school. OCHA estimated that citizens could not use one in four schools because they were damaged, destroyed, or in use as shelters for IDPs or for military purposes. According to UNICEF, 52,500 teachers had left their posts in the first four years of the conflict. It also estimated that 2.4 million schoolchildren between the ages of three and 17 were no longer attending school. Societal pressure for early marriage and childbearing interfered with girls' educational progress, particularly in rural areas, where dropout rates for female students remained high.

According to several reports, Da'esh segregated classrooms (including teachers) by gender, dismissed students for dress code violations, imposed its curriculum on teachers, and closed private schools and educational centers. According to local sources, Da'esh forces prevented young women in Raqqa governorate from traveling to complete their university exams. Da'esh also banned several basic education subjects, such as chemistry.

While Palestinians and other noncitizens, including stateless Kurds, could generally send their children to school and universities, stateless Kurds were ineligible to receive a degree documenting their academic achievement.

Child Abuse: The country lacked a formal law protecting children from abuse. There were reports of government forces sexually assaulting, torturing, detaining, and killing children (see sections 1.a., 1.b., 1.c., and 1.g.). HRW reported that government teachers and principals interrogated and, in some cases, beat students who expressed antigovernment sentiments. Additionally, the United Nations, HRW, and local news sources reported that government forces used children as human shields.

Da'esh subjected children to extremely harsh punishments, including execution (see section 1.g.).

<u>Early and Forced Marriage</u>: The legal age for marriage is 18 for men and 17 for women. A boy or girl who is 15 or older may marry if a judge deems both parties willing and "physically mature," and if the fathers or grandfathers of both parties consent. Although underage marriage declined considerably in past decades, it was common and occurred in all communities, albeit in greater numbers in rural and less developed regions. The media and NGOs reported that early marriage, particularly among girls, increased among Syrian refugee populations.

Da'esh systematically abducted and sexually exploited Yezidi girls in Iraq and transported them to Syria for systematic rape and forced marriage (see section 1.g. and section 6, Women).

<u>Female Genital Mutilation/Cutting</u>: See Women above.

<u>Sexual Exploitation of Children</u>: The age of sexual consent, in accordance with the law, is 15. Premarital sex is illegal, but observers reported authorities did not enforce the law. Rape of a child under the age of 15 is punishable by up to 21 years in prison. There were no reports of government prosecution of child rape cases.

Media and NGOs claimed that sexual exploitation of girls under the age of 15 remained widespread. In refugee communities some families reportedly prostituted young women and girls due to economic desperation. There were also reports that local government officials and aid workers sexually exploited women and girls in refugee camps.

The penal code stipulates penalties for those found guilty of certain forms of child abuse associated with trafficking crimes, including kidnapping and forced prostitution, both of which carry a penalty of up to three years in prison. The law considers child pornography a trafficking crime, but the penalties for child pornography were set at the local level with "appropriate penalties." It was also unclear if there had been any prosecutions for child pornography or if the law was enforced.

<u>International Child Abductions</u>: The country is not a party to the 1980 Hague Convention on the Civil Aspects of International Child Abduction. See the Department of State's *Annual Report on International Parental Child Abduction* at <u>travel.state.gov/content/childabduction/en/legal/compliance.html</u>.

Anti-Semitism

NGOs estimated fewer than 20 Jews remained in the country. According to the media and the Syrian American Council, in 2014 government forces destroyed the Eliyahu Hanabi synagogue, the country's oldest, in an artillery attack on Jobar, a rebel-held neighborhood in Damascus. Government and opposition forces accused each other of burning and looting the Jobar synagogue.

The national school curriculum did not include materials on tolerance education or the Holocaust.

Trafficking in Persons

See the Department of State's *Trafficking in Persons Report* at www.state.gov/j/tip/rls/tiprpt/.

Persons with Disabilities

The law prohibits discrimination against persons with disabilities and seeks to integrate them into the public-sector workforce, but the government did not effectively enforce these provisions. The law protects persons with disabilities from discrimination in education, access to health care, or provision of other state services, and it reserves 4 percent of government-sector jobs and 2 percent of private-sector jobs for persons with disabilities. Private businesses are eligible for tax exemptions after hiring persons with disabilities. The law does not address specific disabilities. Syria ratified the Convention on the Rights of Persons with Disabilities (CPRD) and the CPRD's optional protocol that include language regarding prohibition of discrimination against persons with physical, sensory, intellectual, and mental disabilities. They also include language on protecting persons with disabilities from discrimination in air travel and other transportation, as well as in the judicial system. There is no indication that the laws were amended to reflect protections contained in the CPRD and the optional protocol.

Authorities did not fully document the number of persons with disabilities, but the conflict negatively affected persons with disabilities and increased their numbers through injuries. The SNHR reported the deaths of hundreds of citizens with pre-existing health conditions who could not access medical facilities due to conflict-related travel restrictions, including both government and extremist checkpoints. In other instances, government blockades prevented the movement of medical supplies and persons to opposition-held areas and prevented persons with medical needs from seeking appropriate treatment.

The government did not effectively work to provide access for persons with disabilities to buildings, communication, or information. Along with their peers, the conflict increasingly hampered the ability of children with disabilities to attend primary and secondary school in addition to seeking higher education.

The Ministry of Social Affairs and Labor is responsible for assisting persons with disabilities and worked through dedicated charities and organizations to provide assistance.

National/Racial/Ethnic Minorities

As in previous years, the government actively restricted national and ethnic minorities from conducting traditional, religious, and cultural activities. The Kurdish population, citizens and noncitizens, faced official and societal discrimination and repression as well as government-sponsored violence. Government forces arrested, detained, and reportedly tortured numerous Kurdish activists during the year.

The government continued to limit the use and teaching of the Kurdish language. It also restricted publication of books and other materials in Kurdish, Kurdish cultural expression, and at times the celebration of Kurdish festivals. Authorities continued enforcement of a 2009 government rule requiring that at least 60 percent of the words on signs in shops and restaurants be in Arabic (see section 2.a.).

Clashes between Kurdish groups and Da'esh continued during the year. In April residents of Tal Abyad accused Kurdish forces of forcing them out of the town after liberating it in 2015 from Da'esh. Some media and local human rights activists reported that residents in Manbij raised similar concerns after the Syrian Democratic Forces (composed mostly of Kurdish fighters) liberated the city in August.

The Alawite community, to which Bashar Asad belongs, enjoyed privileged status throughout the government and dominated the state security apparatus and military leadership. Nevertheless, the government reportedly also targeted Alawite opposition activists for arbitrary arrest, torture, detention, and killing. Extremist opposition groups targeted Alawite communities on several occasions for their perceived progovernment stance.

Acts of Violence, Discrimination, and Other Abuses Based on Sexual Orientation and Gender Identity

The penal code prohibits homosexual relations, defined as "carnal relations against the order of nature," and provides for at least three years' imprisonment for violations. The law specifically criminalizes any sexual act that is "contrary to nature." In previous years police used this charge to prosecute lesbian, gay, bisexual, transgender, and intersex (LGBTI) individuals. There were no reports of prosecutions under the law during the year, although NGO reports indicated the government arrested dozens of gay men and lesbians over the past several years on charges, such as abusing social values; selling, buying, or consuming illegal drugs; and organizing and promoting "obscene" parties.

Although there were no known domestic NGOs focused on LGBTI matters, there were several online networking communities, including an online LGBTI-oriented magazine. Human rights activists reported there was overt societal discrimination based on sexual orientation and gender identity in all aspects of society. There were also reports of extremist groups threatening LGBTI activists.

Local media reported numerous instances in which security forces used accusations of homosexuality as a pretext to detain, arrest, and torture civilians. The frequency of such instances was difficult to determine, since police rarely reported their rationale for arrests. Furthermore, social stigma prevented many victims of such abuse from coming forward, even when accusations were false. In previous years photographs and videos appeared showing Da'esh pushing men suspected of "being gay" from rooftops in Raqqa governorate or stoning them to death. According to Outright International, on May 7, Da'esh's media office issued a "photo report about the imposition of sharia punishment" on those suspected of belonging to the LGBTI community. The photographs included images of a boy pushed from the top of a building.

HIV and AIDS Social Stigma

There were no reports of violence or discrimination against persons with HIV/AIDS, but human rights activists believed such cases were widely underreported. The government, World Bank, and World Health Organization did not maintain current data on the number of persons infected with HIV/AIDS living in the country. Observers, however, expected the HIV/AIDS rate of infection to rise with increased sexual violence in the country.

Section 7. Worker Rights

a. Freedom of Association and the Right to Collective Bargaining

While the law provides for the right to form and join unions, conduct legal labor strikes, and bargain collectively, there were excessive restrictions on these rights. The law prohibits antiunion discrimination, but the law also allows employers to fire workers at will.

The law requires all unions to belong to the government-affiliated General Federation of Trade Unions (GFTU). Restrictions on freedom of association also included fines and prison sentences for illegal strikes. The government could impose forced labor as punishment on individuals who caused "prejudice to the general production plan." The law prohibits strikes involving more than 20 workers in certain sectors, including transportation and telecommunication, or strike actions resembling public demonstrations.

The law requires that government representatives be part of the bargaining process in the public sector, and the Ministry of Social Affairs and Labor could object to, and refuse to register, any agreements concluded. The labor code and relevant protections do not apply to workers covered under the civil service law, under which employees neither have nor considered to need collective bargaining rights. The labor code does not apply to foreign domestic servants, agricultural workers, NGO employees, or informal-sector workers. There are no legal protections for self-employed workers, although they comprised a significant proportion of the total workforce. Foreign workers may join the syndicate representing their profession but may not run for elected positions, with the exception of Palestinians, who may serve as elected officials in unions.

The government did not enforce applicable laws effectively or make any serious attempt to do so during the year.

The Baath Party dominated the GFTU, and Baath Party doctrine stipulates that its quasi-official constituent unions protect worker rights. The GFTU president was a senior member of the Baath Party, and he and his deputy could attend cabinet meetings on economic affairs. In previous years the GFTU controlled most aspects of union activity, including which sectors or industries could have unions. It also had the power to disband union governing bodies. Union elections were generally free of direct GFTU interference, but successful campaigns usually required membership in the Baath Party. Because of the GFTU's close ties to the government, the right to bargain collectively did not exist in practical terms. Although the law provides for collective bargaining in the private sector, past government repression dissuaded most workers from exercising this right.

There was little information available on employer practices with regard to antiunion discrimination. Unrest and economic decline during the year caused many workers to lose their private-sector jobs, giving employers the stronger hand in disputes.

b. Prohibition of Forced or Compulsory Labor

The law does not prohibit all forms of forced or compulsory labor, and such practices existed. For example, authorities can sentence convicted prisoners to hard labor, although according to the International Labor Organization (ILO), authorities seldom enforced such a sentence. There was little information available on government efforts to enforce relevant laws during the year.

The PYD-affiliated Kurdish security forces reportedly captured unknown numbers of men and women between the ages of 18 and 30 at checkpoints and from residences in Kurdish areas and compelled them to fight for the YPG. Extremist fighters, including Da'esh, reportedly forced, coerced, or fraudulently recruited some foreigners, including migrants from Central Asia, children, and western women to join them.

Syria was a destination and transit country for women and children trafficked for commercial sexual exploitation and forced labor. Penalties for trafficking specify a minimum of seven years in prison and a fine of one to three million pounds ($4,654 to $13,963). The government did not fully comply with the minimum standards for the elimination of trafficking and was not making significant efforts to do so.

Following the February 2015 Da'esh incursion into Assyrian villages in al-Hasakah, Da'esh captured approximately 230 Assyrian Christians, forcing several women into sexual slavery. All appeared to have been freed as of February. Da'esh also abducted thousands of Yezidi women and girls from Iraq and forcibly brought them to Syria, where they experienced systematic rape, forced marriage, domestic servitude, and sexual violence. According to the COI, Da'esh restricted medical professionals' work and in some cases forced doctors to stop working in public hospitals or private clinics and instead work for Da'esh to treat its combatants.

Also see the Department of State's *Trafficking in Persons Report* at
www.state.gov/j/tip/rls/tiprpt/.

c. Prohibition of Child Labor and Minimum Age for Employment

The labor law provides for the protection of children from exploitation in the
workplace. The minimum age for most types of nonagricultural labor is 15 or the
completion of elementary schooling, whichever occurs first, and the minimum age
for employment in industries with heavy work is 17. Parental permission is
required for children younger than 16 to work. Children under 18 may work no
more than six hours a day and may not work overtime or during night shifts,
weekends, or on official holidays. The law specifies that authorities should apply
"appropriate penalties" to violators. Restrictions on child labor do not apply to
those who work in family businesses and do not receive a salary.

There was little publicly available information on enforcement of child labor laws.
The government generally did not make significant efforts to prevent or eliminate
child labor. Independent information and audits regarding government
enforcement were not available.

Child labor occurred in the country in both informal sectors, such as begging,
domestic work, and agriculture, as well as in positions related to the conflict, such
as lookouts, spies, and informants. Conflict-related work subjected children to
significant dangers of retaliation and violence. Prior to the start of protests in
2011, there was progress in removing children from bonded agricultural labor
organizations and street begging schemes, although the outbreak of civil war halted
that progress. The ILO noted that Syrian refugee children in places such as Jordan
and Lebanon were especially vulnerable to forced labor such as begging, and some
children were the sole breadwinners in their families.

The government continued to forcibly recruit and use child soldiers; it also failed
to protect and prevent children from recruitment and use by government, armed
opposition forces, and designated terrorist organizations such as Da'esh.

Organized begging rings particularly continued to subject children displaced within
the country to forced labor. According to UNICEF, six million children were in
urgent need of life-saving assistance. UNICEF also reported that fighting
destroyed, damaged, or occupied one in every four schools, and more than two
million children were out of school. Save the Children and UNICEF reported that

more than 75 percent of the country's households had children working rather than attending school since the civil war began.

d. Discrimination with Respect to Employment and Occupation

The constitution prohibits discrimination against persons on the basis of race, color, marital status, belief, political opinion, trade union membership, nationality, descent, or disability. The constitution prohibits discrimination based on gender, although personal status and penal laws continued to discriminate. The constitution does not address discrimination based on sexual orientation, age, or HIV-positive status. Since the government legally prohibits homosexuality (see section 6, Acts of Violence, Discrimination, and Other Abuses Based on Sexual Orientation and Gender Identity), many persons faced discrimination due to their sexual orientation. There were no reports of government activities to encourage participation or prevent discrimination against persons with disabilities. Discrimination in employment and occupation occurred with respect to certain ethnic groups (see section 6, National/Racial/Ethnic Minorities).

e. Acceptable Conditions of Work

The law divides the public-sector monthly minimum wage into five levels based on job type or level of education, varying between 9,765 and 14,760 Syrian pounds ($45 to $69) per month. Benefits included compensation for meals, uniforms, and transportation. Most public-sector employees relied on bribery to supplement their income. Private-sector companies usually paid much higher wages, with lower-end wage rates semiofficially set by the government and employer organizations. Many workers in the public and private sectors took additional manual jobs or relied on their extended families to support them.

The public-sector workweek was 35 hours, and the standard private-sector workweek was 40 hours, excluding meals and rest breaks. Hours of work could increase or decrease, based on the industry and associated health hazards. The law provides for at least one meal or rest break totaling no less than one hour per day. Employers must schedule hours of work and rest such that workers do not work more than five consecutive hours or 10 hours per day in total. Employers must provide premium pay for overtime work.

The government set occupational safety and health standards. The labor code includes provisions mandating that employers take appropriate precautions to protect workers from hazards inherent to the nature of work. The law did not protect workers who chose to remove themselves from situations that endangered their health or safety from losing their employment.

The Ministry of Social Affairs and Labor is responsible for enforcing the minimum wage and other regulations pertaining to acceptable conditions of work. The Ministries of Health and of Social Affairs and Labor designated officials to inspect worksites for compliance with health and safety standards. Workers could lodge complaints about health and safety conditions with special committees established to adjudicate such cases. Wage and hour regulations as well as occupational health and safety rules do not apply to migrant workers, rendering them more vulnerable to abuse.

There was little information on government enforcement of labor laws or working conditions during the year. There were no health and safety inspections reported, and even previously routine inspections of tourist facilities such as hotels and major restaurants no longer occurred. The enforcement of labor laws was lax in both rural and urban areas, since many inspector positions were vacant due to the violence. For example, there were only 20 inspectors for the agricultural sector to cover more than 10,000 workplaces. Penalties were not sufficient to deter violations.

Foreign workers, especially domestic workers, remained vulnerable to exploitative conditions. For example, the law does not legally entitle foreign female domestics to the same wages as Syrian domestics. The violence affected foreign workers, some of whom found it difficult to leave the country. The Ministry of Social Affairs and Labor is in charge of regulating employment agencies responsible for providing safe working conditions for migrant domestic workers, but the scope of oversight was unknown. In large cities Asian domestic workers sometimes overstayed their visas and continued to work in the country for years. The continued unrest resulted in the large-scale voluntary departure of foreign workers as demand for services significantly declined.